AFTER MANY DAYS

My Life as a Spy and
Other Grand Adventures

Shirley H. Perry

HELLGATE PRESS   ASHLAND, OREGON

AFTER MANY DAYS

©2010 Shirley H. Perry

Published by Hellgate Press (An imprint of L&R Publishing, LLC)

Hellgate Press
PO Box 3531
Ashland, OR 97520

www.hellgatepress.com

Editor: Harley B. Patrick
Interior design: L.I. Redding
Cover and map design: Rob Perry
Cover photo: Marie Hendricks

Library of Congress Cataloging-in-Publication Data

Perry, Shirley H., 1929-
After many days : my life as a spy and other grand adventures / Shirley H. Perry. -- 1st ed.
  p. cm.
 ISBN 978-1-55571-672-1
1. Perry, Shirley H., 1929- 2. Women spies--United States--Biography.
3. United States. Central Intelligence Agency--Biography. 4. Women adventurers--United States--Biography. 5. Women travelers--United States--Biography. I. Title.
 CT275.P578 A3
 327.12092--dc22

Printed and bound in the United States of America
First edition 10 9 8 7 6 5 4 3 2 1

*For Andrea, for Rob
and for Marilyn*

*Cast thy bread upon the waters:
for thou shalt find it after many days.*

Ecclesiastes 11: 1

Contents

Central Intelligence Agency
Publications Review Board

4 August 1999

Ms. Shirley Hendricks Perry
5 Myrtle Street, #3
Boston, MA 02114-4119

Dear Ms. Perry:

The Publications Review Board has received your three manuscripts. Before
we begin a review however, we must verify the author's employment, and we have
not been able to locate your records. Please supply us with your Social Security
number so we can make another search. Were you using the above name during the
time of your employment?

Your cooperation in this review process is appreciated.

Sincerely yours,

Chairman, Publications Review Board

OCCUPIED
AUSTRIA

1945-1955

Poland

Prague

Czechoslovakia

West
Germany

Soviet
Zone

Munich

U.S.
Zone

Linz

Vienna

French Zone

Switz.

British
Zone

Graz

Hung.

Italy

Venice

Yugoslavia

Adriatic
Sea

N

0   50   100
Scale   in   Miles

I Spy

*From Stettin in the Baltic to Trieste in the Adriatic,
an iron curtain has descended across the Continent*
—Winston Churchill

"**O**h, no! No! That can't be right!" My stomach churned. This could not be happening! I was trying not to panic, but was very close to tears. So much for the sophisticated feeling I had when I walked up the ramp and stepped aboard the sleek, new ocean liner, the SS *United States*, that would be taking me to Europe.

I'd had a wonderful time in New York City the day before, topped off with an evening at the theater. Seeing a play on Broadway was an experience like none other for this drama major from the Midwest. I'd had the "dog seat"—K-9—that the usher assured me was the lucky seat in the house. I was thinking that nothing could go wrong given such a fortuitous start to my overseas adventure.

But go wrong it did. The purser had just informed me that my steamer trunk was not on the ship's manifest. I tried to figure out why since I knew from the bill of lading that it had been shipped in plenty of time. It had to have arrived, I insisted.

"I'm sorry, miss, but I have no record of it," the purser replied, not too patiently.

"What can I do? It's got to be here. Can I look for it?" I was desperate. All my worldly goods were in that trunk. I couldn't arrive in Europe with a just a suitcase!

In fact, I couldn't even sail with just a suitcase. My whole assignment abroad with the CIA was in jeopardy.

"Well, yes, you could get off the ship and go down to the loading dock and see if you can find it," the purser offered, having no better suggestion. "But, the baggage area is as big as a football field. Start with the first class section."

Of course I'll start there, I thought, since I have a first class ticket, but that seemed too smart-alecky to say, so I simply turned away and headed for the gangplank. Then it hit me. If I couldn't find my trunk in the first class section I would have to troop through the all the other sections. The ship was sailing in an hour and a half. Did I have enough time? What about Tod? He was coming to bid me bon voyage and had promised to bring along a bottle of champagne. What about my happy, carefree send off?

It was a warm September day and along with my confidence, my hair was unraveling. I had started out with a perfect pageboy and looked quite smart in my gray flannel suit, with its flared skirt and fitted, double-breasted jacket. My costume was completed with while gloves and a brand new purse but now I crammed the gloves into my purse, took out a handkerchief to blot my perspiration, and set out to survey the loading dock.

The baggage was organized in large sections marked off alphabetically. I walked up and down row after row, looking for my trunk under each letter—it could be anywhere! I saved my closest scrutiny for the letter H. Along with Shirley Hendricks, it seemed as if most of the passengers had a last name beginning with H. I stood on tiptoe to peer across the fence-like barrier and tried to check out every piece of luggage. Nothing. I was sweating as I approached the end of the H's. No trunk in sight.

I was plowing on to the next row when I spotted a grouping set somewhat apart from the rest. It was a collection of expensive designer trunks and suitcases and hatboxes belonging to someone else whose last name also began with H. One of the handsome trunks was right next to the fence and I could read the name on a tag: Rita Hayworth! Despite my anxiety, I had to pause to admire the ensemble—all the pieces in beautiful tan leather with brass trim. This pleasing picture was marred by a most discordant note, however, for there, in the midst of this elegant assemblage, like the proverbial black sheep of the flock, stood my plain, black steamer trunk! The lost was found! I was overjoyed. As I raced back on board I wondered how the dock workers could have made such a glaring mistake.

The purser assured me my trunk would be plucked out of Miss Hayworth's pile and put in the hold under my name. I was finally free to enjoy a glass of champagne with Tod who had been searching frantically for me and looked as wilted as I and as worried as I had been. Predictably, the sparkling drink and the festive atmosphere quickly changed our mood and we had time for a fast tour of the salons on the promenade deck before the signal sounded for all visitors to debark. That warning suddenly seemed so final and somehow ominous as we kissed goodbye and promised to write.

There was music, confetti and a great swirl of people milling about as the ship inched away from the dock, bound for Le Harve. I was caught up in all the excitement but when we sailed past the Statue of Liberty, the realization that I was leaving the United States hit home. I was going so far away. What would await me? Would I be homesick, would I be happy? I was teary-eyed and felt quite alone as I watched the great lady fade into the distance.

But how could anyone be sad aboard such a glamorous ship? I was cheered at finding flowers from my family in my stateroom, and some from Tod and a college beau, too, along with cables from friends and a special delivery letter from a beloved aunt. And, besides, I had met two good looking exchange students who were returning to Germany after studying in Indiana. Clem and Otto and I had a great time exploring the ship together, from the boiler room to the top deck, and they invited me to the dances down in third class where there was plenty of beer and pretzels and lots of loud music. Up in first class, we dined on Beluga caviar, bisque of lobster royale and could choose from ten entrees and countless desserts. I ate it all up.

My accommodations were very nice but I was scarcely in my stateroom except to change clothes and sleep so I seldom saw my roommate; in fact, I don't even remember who she was. The *United States* was the world's largest and fastest ship and whisked us across the ocean in five days. The crossing was an incomparable experience and at Le Havre I boarded the boat train in high spirits. On the ride to the Gare St. Lazare in Paris, I happened to share a compartment with Elia Kazan. What a happy happenstance for this theater buff to sit across from a famous director of stage and screen and chat with him. Though I can't recall what words were said, I can't forget the feeling of inclusiveness I had and the feeling of being so grown up.

I spent a couple of delightful days seeing the sights in the City

of Light and made a visit to the apartment of two charming
French women where my Uncle Tommy lived while he was sta-
tioned in Paris during WWII. He had worked for the Illinois
Central Railroad in Alton, IL, and was in the Army Transportation
Department, Second Military Railway Service that landed at Utah
Beach in Normandy eleven days after D-Day. My uncle was part
of the group that struggled to transport a dinky steam locomotive
across the sand and up to the top of the cliff. My cousin, Dave
Byrnes, remembers his dad saying they finally got the engine to
Cherbourg where they found a railroad track and then used the
engine to pull freight cars of supplies. This effort had proved to be
extremely difficult because none of the French railroad equipment was compatible with the U.S. engine. Dave has a newspaper
article with a photograph showing his dad placing a U.S. flag on
the first steam locomotive to cross from France into Germany! On
25 Feb 1945, his headquarters in Paris closed as of 2400 hours
and my uncle returned to the United States.

In 1952, right before I left for Europe, Uncle Tommy gave me
the address of Madame Sauvage and Madame Villeneuve who
lived on the *rue Hippolyte Lebas* not far from the St. Georges
metro stop on the *rue Notre Dame de Lorette* on the way to
Montmartre. Now I made my way there. I had phoned first—it
was a brief and probably to them an hilarious conversation, given
my rudimentary capability *en Francais*, but I succeeded in identi-
fying myself and announcing my imminent arrival after declining,
I hoped politely, Mme.Villeneuve's directions that had begun to
confuse me. With the aide of a trusty city map, I managed to find
their place without too much delay.

The mesdames, two lively little ladies, were gracious hostesses
and served café au lait and cake and peppered me with questions

about my uncle, whose photograph they still had prominently displayed on an end table. Clearly, they adored him—and missed him—and I did my best to fill them in on the developments in his family informing them that Uncle Tommy now had a daughter in addition to his young son and that he was back working on the railroad in Alton, Illinois.

I left their cozy apartment feeling less strange in this celebrated foreign city and planned to come back one day. There was so much yet to see, so much more to learn about this culture that dated back to 55 BC! I was dizzy with the prospect. Everything was new and exciting to me, someone still impressed with the size and history of St. Louis. I have kept the card those dear ladies sent me my first Christmas in Europe for they were my first acquaintances abroad, they had welcomed me to the Continent.

It was time to travel on to my final destination, Vienna, a city that would prove to be more exciting than Paris saturated as it was with intrigue and espionage. I caught the fabled Orient Express for a ride through the magnificent Alps to Salzburg, Austria. There, I transferred to the daily U.S. military train affectionately dubbed "The Mozart Express" that ran through the Soviet Zone and was exempted from search by occupation agreements. It took me safely through the Zone to Vienna.

Austria had been divided into four zones of occupation in 1945. The Russians occupied the eastern zone, an area that ran west to the Enns River and included Vienna, the capital. The U.S. zone started at the Enns River and went west to the German border and included Salzburg and Linz. The British and French occupation areas ran along southern Austria, from west to east.

Vienna itself was some ninety miles inside the Soviet zone. Like the country, Vienna was a divided city. There were five sectors, one for each of the occupying powers and a fifth, the First District or Innere Stadt, was an International Sector governed and guarded by each of the occupation forces on a monthly, rotating basis. U.S. Army regulations prohibited the taking of photographs of Soviet soldiers, equipment or installations. The only exception to this ban was on the day each month when control of the International Sector changed. Then, photographs could be taken of the Soviet personnel present at the Palace of Justice where the change-over ceremonies were held. While people could move freely within the Vienna city limits, few Westerners and NO CIA employees entered the Soviet sector.

Vienna! The easternmost outpost of the West. It is actually east of Prague and far behind the Iron Curtain Churchill christened when he spoke at Westminster College in Fulton, Missouri, in March of 1946. His description of the split between East and West came to symbolize the schism of the Cold War era that followed the end of the shooting war. Although World War II was over, a new battle between ideologies had begun, one that was fought clandestinely by spies on the field of espionage.

After the defeat of Germany in May 1945, Stalin stopped all cooperation with the Western intelligence agencies and, by 1946, the major espionage services faced the new fight. Europe was swarming with countless agents—the supply swelling to meet the demand. In Austria, and especially in Vienna, where people were hard pressed to make an honest living, spying became a supplemental source of income.

Given its location, Vienna was also an ideal destination for defectors and refugees escaping Czechoslovakia or Hungary as well as a launching pad for Western agents heading for Eastern Europe. It was also swarming with hundreds of Russians—military, diplomatic and intelligence personnel who were the "hard targets" that CIA headquarters tasked the station to recruit. The city was also full of operatives from the Western intelligence agencies as well. Vienna became, actually, an intelligence battleground as we fought to penetrate the Soviet establishment. We had such a paucity of information on the USSR that even a private in the Red Army would have been a welcome source, for up until the early '50s, it was believed that neither the CIA nor any other Western espionage agency had been able to recruit a single Russian official.*

Enter one Lt. Col. Pyotr Popov, a case officer on the Strategic Intelligence Desk of the GRU, the elite Soviet Military Intelligence Directorate, under cover in Vienna. And, one Shirley Hendricks, an assistant on the Soviet Desk of the CIA station in Vienna.

Upon graduation from Washington University in St. Louis, I'd been awarded the faculty prize for outstanding senior and, along with that, a graduate fellowship. Armed with the fellowship and my Phi Beta Kappa key, I set out on an uncertain future, enrolling as a graduate student in the psychology department at my alma mater because I didn't know what else to do. The choice was not one I was really enamored with and I soon became bored and uninspired.

I also needed a part-time job to make ends meet, so one day when I was perusing the bulletin board at the employment office I spied a cryptic notice that intrigued me. I went inside to quiz Mrs. Settle, the sole employee, about it. She was uncharacteristically uninformative.

---

*William Hood, *Mole* (New York: W.W. Norton & Company, 1982, p.28).

Lowering her voice, she told me in conspiratorial tones only that it was an interesting government job, then she opened the top drawer of her desk and fished out a fifteen-page application form. She handed it to me without further comment. It was labeled a "personal history statement" that turned out to be far more than a statement, but very personal. I labored over it and finally sent it off—to the Central Intelligence Agency! The very act seemed daring and the prospect of working in Washington, D.C., was very exciting. With the optimism of youth, I quit my graduate program and went back home, in nearby Illinois, to await my preliminary clearance, buoyed up by expectations of adventure and independence.

It took all summer. But at last I was off to Washington where I spent three months in a make-work typing pool, referred to as typing pool hell by those of us swimming around in that limbo, waiting for my top secret clearance to come through. I had booked a room in a women's hotel in Washington and stayed there, at "menopause manor" as it was called, until I met several other new CIA recruits who, like I, wanted a place of their own. Together we moved into a large home off Dupont Circle where we were ensconced on the top floor, in four small rooms that were formerly the maids' quarters. There was a large living room and an adequate kitchen and, best of all, access to the roof where we could sun and see all over the city.

The last hurdle for clearance was the polygraph test. I was apprehensive because I had been receiving unsolicited copies of the Communist Party's *Daily Worker* when living in St. Louis and had a hard time getting it stopped. So, when I was asked, right before the test, if I had anything to explain, wow, did I! My palms were still sweating when I was hooked up to the machine, but I passed and went on to my appointed job, one that turned out to be the choicest assignment of all—to the Soviet Desk—the highest priority operation in all of the covert side of "the company," as we called the agency. It was pure good luck.

I spent about a year in Washington, working in the old "temporary" Army barracks on the Mall and learning a lot about the Soviet Union and about tradecraft and espionage in general. The highlight of our indoctrination was a session with none other that Alan Dulles himself—he of OSS fame and the first head of the CIA—who addressed the new recruits at length.

Work days on the Desk were busy ones, and so interesting. I was often running name traces, hurrying along the length of the interconnected temps to the building at the farthest end, then delving into cabinets crammed with the files on everyone whose name or organization had ever come to the attention of the CIA. So many of the folders were filled with flimsy, onion-skin paper, the third or fourth copy of some original document whose fuzzy print made reading a challenge. But I found that piecing together the references to get a clear picture of a subject and reporting it back to the field was quite satisfying, not to mention important. I liked filing in my office, too; it was a chance to see information on the current operations and eventually I was able to read in on certain cases.

Soon I had another bit of pure good luck. I was recruited by the head of the Soviet Desk in Vienna, Peter, to transfer there to be his assistant. I was thrilled. My parents, however, were not. While my cover story identified me simply as a typist, my parents knew I was with the CIA, but they had no idea about the real nature of the work I was doing, nor did anyone else. It was just as well.

The early '50s were an exciting and challenging time at the Vienna station. Its Soviet operations branch was occupied with compiling biographical data on Russian targets; such files were the backbone of good intelligence gathering. Ideally, this data should include photos that could be shown to double agents to confirm a subject's identity and other data. The chief of operations, William Hood, concluded that the station needed a mug book and our technical department cleverly devised a way to assemble one.

The station's tech man found a small 35mm camera called "the Robot" in a Viennese camera shop. It had a spring that when wound would automatically advance the film and cock the camera after each exposure. This was placed inside our car's talisman, a little stuffed tiger. Since it was common practice for drivers to display such mascots in the rear windows of their cars, it was a perfect camouflage for our purposes. Then, our non-descript car was parked in the *Innere Stadt* near the crosswalk the Soviets used to go from their hotel headquarters to a favorite restaurant across the street. Nearby, a case officer hung around; he had a concealed radio that could trigger the camera when a desired target started to cross the street.*

We were able to collect dozens of photos this way and slowly our case officers identified the subjects by showing them to agents working in the vicinity of the Soviet installations and using other sources. And this is where I came in—I was one of two keepers of this mug shot book, analyzing the various bits of information sent in from the case officers and writing up each subject's biographi-

---

*Ibid, pp. 74-76.

cal data. Then I would file the subject's information in the proper *Leitz* notebook according to the Soviet organization he worked for. This took time and a lot of it was speculation for without an inside source, we couldn't be certain how reliable our analysis was. But now the station had an inside source—Popov!

Soon after my arrival, the station was focused on the recruitment of Lt. Col Popov. He provided the CIA with the innermost secrets of Soviet intelligence and military developments. Popov was in the GRU, which was charged with military and foreign intelligence. He was a classic double agent—*our* double agent. And now, we could vet our mug books. As it turned out, we did pretty well. According to Hood, a third of the case officers cited by Popov were in our files, correctly identified as GRU operatives and now, with the information he gave us, we had the cover names, true names, and specific operational assignments of the ranking GRU staff in Vienna. We were getting to our hard targets.*

I was getting the lay of the land as well. I'd been billeted at the Cottage Hotel, where Americans were put up upon arrival, and stayed there until I found a roommate and a house in the city. In the hotel at the same time was a CIA family also awaiting housing. The husband was most welcoming. In fact, he took it upon himself to stop by my room in the evenings and inquire after my well being. I politely let him in at first but when he started to talk about burning our candles at both ends I realized he wasn't trying to quote poetry but was propositioning me. It wasn't hard to keep my door locked and be unavailable and, fortunately, I moved out shortly thereafter. Maybe he had better luck with the next new arrival.

Not long after that, one of men at the office offered me a ride

---

*Ibid, p. 77.

home from work. The weather was nasty and I gratefully accepted. We were having an animated conversation and I was enjoying his company immensely, when, all of a sudden, as he drove under an overpass, he displayed more than witty repartee. This conversation stopper left me tongue-tied but I couldn't stop staring. I had a pretty good idea of what he was asking for even though I had always declined such invitations in the past. While I wasn't going to accept now, I also wasn't going to jump out of the car—after all, it was raining...hard. I decided to make light of the situation in hopes he wouldn't feel too embarrassed—never mind my own mortification.

I finally came up with, "Hey, you're going to catch cold." I tried a little laugh.

"Yeah, it's pretty frosty in here," was all he could muster. Certainly not an apology for offending me. I guess I was supposed to be flattered by his magnanimous offer, but I wasn't going to apologize either for not accommodating him. He managed to get the errant party back where it belonged as we drove on, each of us searching for something else to say until, at last, we reached my house. I dashed out and ran for my door. I was soaked, but safe inside.

I dreaded the next day, when I would encounter him at work. We were certain to see each other and we did. We didn't acknowledge each other. This silly behavior went on for a while until one day, when we met in the hall, I couldn't help but smile. He did too. The next time I saw him, we both laughed, relieved. Much later, when he learned I was to be married, he extended his best wishes and told me he'd always have a soft spot in his heart for me. I thanked him but couldn't suppress a knowing smile. He must have been reading my mind for he laughed a little and leaned in to whisper, "And you know what else..." I did indeed.

THANKSGIVING DAY

Spying is a stressful business and none of us at the Vienna station was spared its effects. So two of my colleagues and I planned to get away over a Thanksgiving—my first in Vienna—to Salzburg where one of my girl friends had an invitation to a holiday dinner. None of us had a car and we had decided to take the Mozart when we learned that a company guy was driving through the Soviet zone on Thanksgiving Eve. So we hitched a ride with Boris, setting out in the early evening in this man's dilapidated old car with an unreliable heater. And it was cold, starting to snow, in fact.

We drove by the checkpoint right outside Vienna where our license number and time of entry into the zone were recorded by the U.S. Military Police. This was done in case a car didn't turn up at the exit point in Enns within the allotted time—approximately two hours. In such a case, the MPs would set out to find the tardy travelers. We were to find out how well the system worked for about half way on our journey through the Soviet zone, as we approached the town of Amstettin, the car sputtered and simply rolled to a stop!

Boris cranked and cranked, but it would not start. The chances of working successfully on the old vehicle in the freezing, pitch-dark night on the main road through Soviet territory were slim indeed, so Boris declared he would walk into the town to look for help. This didn't seem smart. Americans, especially those with the CIA, should not be loitering in the zone, and what could he find open at this late hour anyway, I wondered? It was almost eight o'clock. But, off he went while we three huddled together in the back seat and tried to keep warm. Boris eventually returned, without help, of course, and we were pondering our fate when we heard a vehicle approaching.

By now it was snowing hard and we couldn't see who had pulled up. It became abundantly clear in just a few moments though—it was the Soviet patrol. The worst was happening! Before I could contemplate the extent of the trouble we were in, we were ordered out of the car at gun point and into the soldiers' jeep that took us directly to the Soviet *Kommandantura*, a regional Soviet military headquarters, in the town. Our suitcases were left in the broken down car.

There we were locked into two cells—we three women in one, and, we assumed, our male colleague in another, apart from us, where we couldn't see him. If ever an American was picked up by the Soviets in their zone of Austria, he was allowed to make one telephone call to notify friends or family and arrange to get out. CIA employees who had a breakdown in the zone were not to wait until it was discovered that their car was late reaching the checkpoint. The procedure in such an event was to phone, as soon as possible, an emergency duty officer at the Vienna station who, in turn, would phone the Military Police instructing them to go posthaste to the rescue.

Together, we four were allowed one phone call and it appeared that this responsibility would fall to the car's driver; we "girls" were not allowed to call and were ushered straight into our cell. We trusted that Boris made the call and could but sit and wait and pray the MPs would arrive soon.

I'm sure our hosts didn't know whom they had in custody, ostensibly we were just a low-ranking translator and three secretaries, so we did our best to appear as insignificant and unworried as possible. But I was scared when a pimply-faced private entered our cell and sat down on a chair facing the wall-backed wooden bench we three perched on, shifting his AK-47 authoritatively and staring menacingly at us. After this intimidating show of control, he gave us a sideways smile, exposing some really bad teeth. Actually, the look was more like a leer. Carol, one of my companions, was eyeing him with a silly smile of her own. I jabbed her in the ribs.

"Carol, what are you doing?" I said under my breath. "Stop smiling at him! Don't give him any idea that we're at all friendly."

"But if we act friendly, we could get him to bring us something to eat, or some water," she countered.

"And you'd eat something he'd bring us? Besides," I added, trying to sound reasonable and ominous at the same time, "you don't know what he'd expect in return." I could imagine our having to take off our jewelry and watches or empty our purses in payment.

Carol seemed convinced to drop her smiling strategy and we sat for a while in silence. Suddenly, the soldier stood up and started to pace, shifting his rifle from one shoulder to the other. The sound startled us. Kathy, my roommate, was seated on the other side of Carol. She looked worried.

"We've been here for almost three hours now and there's no sign of the MPs," she said, pointing out the obvious, much to our distress. It was close to midnight.

"I hope Boris made the call," I responded. My comment only made us more tense.

I began to wonder what would happen if the MPs didn't come soon. Would the Soviets subject us to hostile interrogations? Would they report our capture to their Soviet superiors, to their intelligence officers? Would they search us? Would we be kept incommunicado? What would they do with Boris? I was conjuring up dire situations and searching for responses, all the while trying to believe that none of these scenarios would happen yet wanting to anticipate the worst.

My pessimistic thoughts were interrupted when the Soviet officer who had been sitting at a desk in the outer part of the large room that housed our cell summoned our guard. The officer looked over at us and conferred with the private. What now? Were my fears going to come true? Are they preparing to take us, one by one, into some dank, dark room to be questioned and threatened? We each had our cover stories straight and had followed procedure so far, but we were tired and hungry—and vulnerable. The officer then dispatched another private out of the room and sent our guard back to us. After a while, the errand boy returned with some sandwiches and tea—for everyone. Our captors weren't completely without compassion, after all. I figured it was safe to eat what the soldiers were wolfing down so we hungrily and gratefully joined them.

After the meal, we three had another concern. With a combination of gestures and a bit of German, we made ourselves understood and were escorted by our gun-toting guard to the WC. This was an experience we wished we could have done without, however, it afforded us a chance to re-enforce a no-talking policy and to give ourselves a pep talk.

Once we were resettled on our wooden bench, the lieutenant entered our cell. Despite my anxiety, I was captivated by the presence of a real Soviet officer. He wasn't just an entry in my mug book, he was the living, breathing enemy—a Communist up close. He appeared increasingly curious about us and asked our names again and what our jobs were. Did he regard us as enemies, too? He spoke to us in halting English and I quickly became apprehensive. We were required to give out only our names and cover organizations, and that's all we did, but what worried me was the thought that he could understand English better than he could speak it. Had he overheard anything significant? He seemed to be fishing for information, but I just shrugged and Carol and Kathy followed suit, playing dumb. I wasn't sure how long we could keep up the charade nor what the consequences would be if the officer became more insistent. I was becoming more and more nervous when, thanks be, I heard a commotion outside. The officer left the cell, making sure the private still had us under guard.

There were loud voices and suddenly, we saw the U.S. MPs and Boris! A Soviet soldier was unlocking our cell and we were rushed out to two waiting jeeps. I think Carol waved goodbye. After picking up our luggage from the abandoned car, which the MPs assured Boris would be towed to a garage, we sped away to the checkpoint. How relieved I was! How refreshing the cold wind felt after the stuffy air in the cell. How thankful I was to be free again to feast with friends on Thanksgiving Day. At the checkpoint, we had to call and wait for our friends to drive out from Salzburg to rescue us. Finally, in the wee hours of the holiday, we went to bed—safe and sound at last.

This brush with the enemy only reinforced my dedication to our mission there and my allegiance to my comrades-in-Cold-War-arms. We were a brave band of intelligence officers stationed behind the Iron Curtain and, together with the families of those who had them, were good friends as well as colleagues. We dined at each other's homes, shared each other's joys and tribulations and, in general, looked out for one another.

And, we partied together. Charades was the rage at many of our parties and the favorite title for acting out was "portion garbled, being serviced." This phrase in a cable from headquarters occurred with maddening frequency and usually appeared in place of the most significant information the cable was expected to relay. It could evoke furious and frustrating reaction among case officers and made for a most dramatic pantomime on the part of the actor who drew that assignment. "Plausible denial" was another oft-acted expression; I never knew if its real use was ever invoked but did know that it could be.

Rank was not a determining factor on our social scene. The chief of station entertained everyone at his home—I've kept an invitation from Jocko R., the station chief when I arrived, for after-dinner drinks. He worked at a different location from the operations personnel who occupied the *Stiftskaserne*, an old American military police office. The station's senior officers always went to the chief's office for meetings, so our paths seldom crossed. However, from time to time, I would see Jocko at the Bristol, the American hotel and watering hole. One time, I was at the news-stand at the hotel looking over the magazines when he approached. I ventured a comment on a particularly disturbing cover story.

"Where there's smoke, there's fire," he replied grimly. Actually, he always seemed a worried man to me the few times I saw him.

Still, while we all knew each other well, we respected the boundaries of privacy and did not become a socially incestuous society living only in the cocoon of community.

We vetted our "outside" friends and contacts and our personal relationships were guided by the same "need to know" credo we assiduously followed in our professional lives. We were not immune, either, to the common afflictions of the human condition—changing relationships. There was the usual grapevine speculation about "who's dating whom," and there were marriages, divorces, and re-couplings, but nothing that derailed the job at hand.

With all the closeness our group experienced, we could have become a contentious ensemble, but we did not. Our mission was the overriding motivation for cooperation and collegiality. There was little of the typical workplace competition but, rather, an enduring esprit that served to unite us all in our common objective.

Sharing all the tensions, successes, and failures of this life behind the Iron Curtain, with its professional demands and personal frustrations, we thought of ourselves as unique. We were, actually, having been recruited especially for this assignment—we were a small collection of talented, calculated risk-taking, dedicated agency employees who became a closely-knit, smoothly operating unit. The male cadre was known as "The Vienna Choir Boys" and while we "girls" weren't specifically included in that sobriquet, we certainly thought of ourselves as part of the team. Together, we were, in fact, the elite corps of intelligence operatives among the many present in Vienna then. There were also the U.S. Army agencies with whom we maintained contact and shared certain information. Allied intelligence organizations had representatives there, too; however, we had little contact with them in the field. And, of course, there were the enemy services that were our targets.

In that four-power city, we with the CIA forged a bond that has lasted for decades. At our reunions, we reminisce about those days and about those who are no longer with us. Those of us who remain share a special connection and I shall always be thankful for that.

Chorus would have been "apt."

EASTER TIME

Soon after the Thanksgiving adventure, when my roommate, Kathy, and I were returning from a ski trip, I met this handsome Army sergeant aboard the Mozart. He was blond and blue-eyed and looked rather disheveled, returning to duty after what I assume had been a heavy weekend away in Salzburg. He and his buddy invited us to share their compartment and, upon our arrival in Vienna, offered to drive us home. I protested, but not too adamantly for it was a long ride on the streetcar, the number 41, that lumbered along the route to our house.

"That would be great, but we live way out in the 19th *Bezirk*."

"No problem, so do we," the sergeant said and smiled.

"Our place is on *Poetzleinsdorferstrasse*."

"So is ours."

"You mean you live in that beautiful place up on the hill?"

"In the VAC villa, yes," said he.

"Then we live across the street from one another!"

How perfect, I decided. A ride home and a prospective boy friend nearby! That elegant villa on the hill, the Vienna Army Corps villa, I later learned, housed the single CIC—the Army's Counter Intelligence Corps—men stationed in Vienna. It was formerly the *Poetzleinsdorfer Schloss*, more a glorious mansion than a castle, set in a sumptuous park designed in the English manner to complement the *Schloss*.

The sergeant's name was Robert Perry and we indeed started to date, just in time to celebrate *Fasching* together. This season of frivolity and frolic before Lent came as a welcome diversion in the midst of the dreary Viennese winter. But Kathy and I had been planning another escape, a trip through the Mid-East over Easter, and we were looking forward to it with great anticipation.

Kathy was the chief architect for our journey, for which I was grateful. She was an excellent organizer and seemed to have more time than I to make the arrangements. She was also a great room-mate—older than I, Lutheran too, and just as eager to see the world. Our paths had crossed in Washington and I was happy to see her again in Vienna. Together we looked for a place to live. We were enamored of the Franz Lehar house that featured the com-poser's grand piano in the spacious living room that opened onto a glorious garden scented with lilacs, but, alas, we could not afford it on our allowances. Instead, we found a delightful cottage in the 19th *Bezirk,* a serendipitous location as it turned out.

The day before we were to leave on our journey, I was bogged down in the office with a tedious task, actually a repeat chore of copying an endless document that a picky, hard-to-please case officer found unsatisfactorily done the first time. I was working frantically to complete some other assignments and resented that I would have to spend at least a couple of hours in the claustro-phobic, clammy room that housed the copy machine. And this machine was an ancient model, nothing like today's zippy copiers. Actually, it was a photocopier in the original sense of the word and it took painfully long to produce duplicate copies. It worked on the basis of thermography and required treated paper. Also, the copies smelled bad and were not durable and, in addition, tended to curl up into tubes. Moreover, I hadn't agreed with the officer's decision to copy the original document in the first place, and, to tell the truth, I resented being dragooned into what I regarded as clerical work I had progressed beyond. Thus it was that I approached this do-over job greatly upset. First, though, I

awkward phrase

rushed to finish the other tasks; I would tackle the copying last.

Of course, everything went wrong with the process, it was getting very late and my frustration built up to the breaking point. I simply could not crank out another page. I marched into the room the case officer shared with others and exploded. I threw the papers on his desk and told him he could finish the job himself! Then I yelled goodbye and stormed out. It was quite an exit. One sympathetic colleague called after me, "Shirley, have a good trip, and do come back!" I didn't answer.

There was no time to bemoan the circumstances of my departure. It was a balmy day in early April and I was off on a fabulous three-week trip to the Middle East! Bob drove Kathy and me to the station where we boarded the Mozart to Salzburg and there we found our train to Italy. It was a sleeper, but we didn't get much sleep, what with the border checks by Austrian and Italian guards, the customs officers and the money exchange official. Nonetheless, we awoke in Venice and were delivered to our hotel by gondola, passing many of the opulent *palazzi* as we poled along that crowded ribbon of water, the Grand Canal. The hotel was a palatial place, erected on piles as was every other structure in the city. The service was superb—we certainly started out first class. On a shopping excursion, I gloried in modeling Venetian lace veils and bought the most beautiful one for my sister's upcoming wedding thinking how I'd love to wear it myself one day. I couldn't resist purchasing an intricately embroidered linen tablecloth as well.

Next, we took a motor boat ride to the glass blowing factory on the autonomous isle of Murano, on the way overtaking a funeral cortege powered by fancily garbed gondoliers transporting flower bedecked coffins to the cemetery island. As our gondolier guide said, "In Venice, it's even romantic to die." On our return, we also saw, among many other sights, the house where Marco Polo lived; the house where Robert Browning died; Barbara Hutton's mansion; the Rialto Bridge; and the Bridge of Sighs. Lord Byron romanticized this elevated course for criminals popularizing the belief that the bridge's name was inspired by the sighs of condemned prisoners glimpsing their last looks as they were led across it from the interrogation rooms in the Doge's Palace to their cells on the other side. On we went to visit the Doge's Palace rising above the *Piazzetta* San Marco and, of course, the Basilica of San Marco decorated with all the riches admirals and merchants could carry off from the Orient in the day. That evening, we dined in the hotel, too tired to oblige evening entertainment offers from a couple of pseudo-suitors.

Next day, up early and on the move, I climbed to the top of the Campanile, the famous brick bell tower in the square, for a panoramic view of the city. It was a clear day and I could see the Lido, the lagoon, and the mainland as far as the Alps, but, strangely enough, none of the myriad canals that snake through the city. Window-shopping tempted us with the fashionable clothing, elegant shoes, glassware, and lace on display. There was time for a delightful concert in St. Mark's Square that afternoon. After picking our way around the pigeon droppings, we joined the crowd sitting at outdoor tables in the soft sunlight and listened to Verdi while sipping the excellent espresso—beautifully bitter and topped with a perfect layer of foaming *crema*. We idled there, lazily watching the passers-by and gawking at the *carabinieri* as they walked along, two by two, resplendent in their uniforms of dark blue with red stripes down the side and white bandoliers across their chests.

Now the real voyage started. In the evening, we took a water

taxi to the pier and boarded the cargo ship *Campidoglia* bound
for Athens with a stop in Brindisi on the Adriatic. A porter ushered us below to our third class accommodations, clean but
Spartan. The food was outstanding and we made friends with the
crew who enjoyed giving us second servings and other extras, like
back issues of *Reader's Digest*, to help pass the time. One of the
sailors even gave me a pair of his pants for I forgot to pack any
slacks. The next day, a glorious Easter morning dawned warm
and clear. The top deck was crammed with cargo, a strange mix of
toilet seats and garlands of garlic, but we didn't want to go below,
to our stuffy dormitory style quarters, so we each chose a "seat,"
festooned ourselves with leis of garlic and sang Easter alleluias to
the high heavens.

After a rough night at sea, we put in at Brindisi at noon and
debarked for a turn around the town. As luck would have it, we
ran into two American Air Force men with whom we explored the
place. They escorted us back to the ship in time for our dinner
aboard, a meal that marked my first—and last—encounter with
squid that I managed to squirt all over myself.

Another warm, sunny day on the water unfolded and ended
with a spectacular sunset. As we steamed along between the
island of Peloponnese and the south coast of Greece, the red ball
of the sun sank slowly behind a jutting mountain while the blue
waters churned white in the ship's wake. There was a small party
on board that night and afterwards we stayed up to watch the ship
maneuver expertly, and very carefully, through the extremely narrow Isthmus of Corinth carved out of rock that rises perpendicu-
larly and threateningly on either side.

The next morning found us docking at Piraeus, the port of
Athens. An Englishman we met on the ship and his Greek host

gave us a tour of the Acropolis. We marveled at the Parthenon, standing since 437 B.C., truly one of the Seven Wonders of the World. What, I wondered, will remain of us and our architecture in millennia to come? That evening we were wined and dined at the home of American friends who invited two agency "eligibles" for Kathy and me. For dinner, there was squid again, but not for me, and octopus, which to my surprise was delicious, then shish kabobs, artichokes, and lots of ouzo. We ended the night in style at a swank nightclub.

We flew next day to Istanbul, hangovers and all. The city was humming with American autos and American products in the store windows. The Turks even copied highway billboard advertising from us—a shame. I was enchanted with the raucous Grand Bazaar and the exotic offerings in the unending rows of stalls. Putting soft slippers over our shoes, we entered the multidomed Blue Mosque, built in the early 1600s and famous for the stunning blue Iznik tiles that grace the tranquil interior. There was also a strong sense of serenity within the much older Haghia Sophia mosque, also a museum, that still displays some of the striking original 6th century Christian mosaics. We were told this structure was valued at one billion dollars—small wonder given that its walls are encrusted with gold and ivory.

On our last morning in Istanbul, we clambered onto a riverboat for a ride up the Bosphorus. It took us thirty miles upstream where we could see, but, of course, could not enter, the Black Sea. There, at the confluence of the waters, we spotted the menacing mines laid to keep us out. The cold winds of Crimea blew through my hair— the chill of the Cold War made real. I felt truly uncomfortable that close to Soviet space and was happy when we turned around and headed back. Up and down the river, we glimpsed old, ornate Ottoman palaces, and newer, imposing summer homes of Embassy officials along side the fashionable resorts for well-to-do vacationers. On the opposite bank, there lay the third of Turkey that is actually in Asia.

At the end of our boat ride, we found ourselves in an inviting resort town where many wealthy mid-Easterners summered. A friend from the boat, a Turkish man who was an English teacher, bought us some delicious, cheesy biscuits at what he maintained was a world famous pastry shop, and together we wandered down to the waterfront where he had some fishermen friends. They were hanging up mackerel to dry but stopped and gave us a royal welcome—the Turks, we found, were most generous and friendly—inviting us to their house and hauling out their best gold-rimmed cups to serve us Turkish coffee with our biscuits.

Everyone wanted to have his picture taken, and we obliged. There was a gaggle of little children playing around the porch where we sat and one particularly endearing urchin posed for us, proudly displaying a dead fish on a string. Our English speaking acquaintance reported that the fishermen had told the child that he was a very lucky boy because his picture would be going to America! Back then, we Americans were warmly welcomed everywhere.

Returning to the city in a cab, costing all of seventy-five cents, our acquaintance suddenly told the driver to stop. He hopped out of the cab and returned with a bouquet of wild Turkish violets he had bought for each of us; they were a rarity, he explained and we clutched them gratefully. Finally back in our hotel, we found a note saying our plane would be departing six hours late, so we had time for a lobster dinner and another trek to the bazaar, although we didn't know the way there from the restaurant. Just then, three U.S. Navy officers strolled by, and, sure enough, they knew. Another of our lucky encounters.

As we walked along, Kathy discovered that one of the men was someone she knew—a Lutheran Navy chaplain whom she had first met in St. Louis when he was at studying at Concordia Seminary there. Small, small world! We spent the rest of the day together and they saw us off at the airport.

We flew from Istanbul to Beirut in three hours and dropped our weary bodies in the best beds we'd slept in since leaving the States. The St. George Hotel was luxurious, with marble floors, a closet where the light came on when the door opened, a balcony overlooking the Mediterranean, and free access to the incomparable beach—and all for $3.00 a night. The next morning, another beautiful, bright day, we hired a car and drove to Baalbek, some fifty miles away, where we visited the ruins of another of the Seven Wonders of the World: the temples of Jupiter, Venus, and Bachus, built by the Romans in the 1st Century. It was an extraordinarily beautiful drive, through the valley with mountains rising on either side, and though the sun was hot, we came upon stretches where people were skiing on nearby slopes. At one place, I reached out of the car window and grabbed a handful of snow from the drifts along the roadside.

We were back in Beirut in time to catch the end of the horse races where the heir apparent of Saudi Arabia, King Ibn Saud's son, was in attendance. We stood just a few feet from his box and took a picture of him, resplendent in Arab garb and headdress, as he presented the trophy to the winner. That evening, our driver took us to an outdoor restaurant on the shores of the Sea where we enjoyed an outstanding Lebanese dinner.

Next morning, we braved the Mediterranean, taking an invigorating dip in the cold azure Sea. In the distance, we could see the snow-covered mountains of the Cedars of Lebanon.

By noon the next day, we were on our way to Damascus, the world's oldest existing city, seventy-five miles from Beirut. Our car would take us across two mountain ranges and, as we climbed, we looked back to watch Beirut disappear from view. The city seemed to sink into the intense blue of the Mediterranean that framed it; the sight was unbelievably lovely.

As soon as we arrived, we hired a guide and proceeded along the Street called Straight to the house where St. Paul was led upon being struck blind and where God told Ananias to find him and restore his sight. The Street called Straight, mentioned in the New Testament, is believed to be the oldest known street in the world, our guide said. He showed us a church, relatively new and built on the site of a prison, that featured the frame of a window through which Paul was supposedly lowered in a basket to make his escape. That story seemed to me to be a tourist truth, for, according to the Bible, Paul was not then imprisoned, although his life was in danger, and he made his exit from Damascus with the help of disciples who lowered him in a basket over the city wall.

We went on to visit the brocade factory where Queen Elizabeth II's wedding gown was made and were told that it took two men one entire day to make just one yard on the hand-operated looms! Here I bought a black and gold brocade evening purse that fast became a favorite. Then we hit the bazaar again for more shopping and, in the evening, went with a group to an Arab nightclub. There were about two hundred local men there and some ten women, all veiled. They couldn't eat or drink because they couldn't raise their veils in public—how boring and frustrating it must have been for them, so burdened by their *burkas*. But I had a great time. Although the music was monotonous, the belly dancing was mesmerizing. Still, I couldn't help but wonder at the women's contrasting clothing—they were either all covered up or almost all uncovered. Obviously, the men could have it both ways.

Up at six the next morning to greet another perfect day. We had breakfast in our room, at the modern Semiramis Hotel, the better to get an early start on our drive to the Holy Land. From the balcony, we watched the passing parade—Arabs with their donkeys; veiled women, some with baskets on their heads; pushcarts; late model American cars—a revealing mixture of the old and new, a combination we saw throughout the Middle East.

We bounced over bad mountain roads in a dilapidated Plymouth, through dry and desert-like country. What a change from the fertile valley of Damascus; how could this be "the Promised Land," I wondered? Along the way, we saw the distinctively dressed riders of the Jordan Army's Arab Legion astride their horses and camels, practicing for their role in the upcoming coronation ceremony of a new king of Jordan. We were warned not to take pictures. Farther on, we spotted Arab nomads grazing their sheep—that certainly looked Biblical. After lunch in Amman, we came to the River Jordan, a small and muddy stream, and were persuaded to buy bottles of its water that a small boy was selling.

Next, we arrived in Jericho. The city, sans walls, sits in a fertile valley, watched over by the Mount of Temptation. It seemed a restful place, at peace after its battles. Elisha's fountain nearby is still a source of water for Jericho's gardens. Just five miles away, the Dead Sea spreads its salty waters over the place where, it's said, Sodom and Gomorrha once stood. We took off our shoes and waded in a little way, refreshing our feet. Mt. Nebo loomed to the east.

Back in the car, we headed through the Judean Desert for Jerusalem, passing Bethany, where Mary and Martha lived, and driving by the inn where the good Samaritan took the man who had fallen among the thieves on the road from Jerusalem to Jericho. On the outskirts of Jerusalem, there stood a large United

Nations building and, opposite, a Russian church established by Czar Alexander III in 1888. Near it was a hospital run jointly by the United Nations and the Lutheran Church.

Gradually, as we neared Jerusalem, the scenery changed, olive trees and plots of green appeared. And, at last, we beheld Jerusalem itself, truly the city on a hill as described in the Bible. It was a sight to remember: the old walled city standing to the left, the Mount of Olives sloping up to the right, and, in the valley in between, groves of olive trees climbing up the hillsides. We went first to our hotel outside the city walls, and stopped only long enough to wash the salt off our feet. Then we were off on a walking tour with our new guide, an Arab named Theo, who proved to be the best so far.

He took us first to the unadorned Church of the Flagellation, inside the Old City, and from there we walked the fourteen Stations of the Cross, along the *Via Dolorosa*, the traditional Way of the Cross, that wound through the busy market streets of the Muslim and Christian quarters to the Church of the Holy Sepulcher. Most Christians venerate this site as that of the death, burial and resurrection of Jesus. How different the reality from my imagination, but did I really expect to see the rolled-away stone still standing outside the tomb on Mt. Calvary? Actually, there seems to be no hill at all, but one can peer through a hole in the church floor next to the altar to see the original stone of the hilltop. In this stone there is a crevice said to have been rent when the earth shook at the time of Christ's crucifixion.

Close by sits Christ's tomb in a small room just high enough for about six people to stand up in. The place where Christ's body had lain buried is marked by a slab of marble, with a small sample of the original rock left to show through an opening. All around were

candles and other decorations representing the trio of faiths allo-
cated designated space in all the holy places in Jerusalem—
Catholic, Greek Orthodox and Armenian. We were allowed to
remain inside the quiet tomb for a moment of meditation. The
whole experience was most moving although I felt like an inter-
loper in such a sacred spot.

Jerusalem was divided by the 1948 war with the much larger
Jewish western sector becoming the capital of the State of Israel
while Jordan annexed the smaller, predominantly Arab eastern
sector that included the Old City. At the time of our visit, the residents of the quarter represented only a tiny percentage of
Jerusalem's Jewish population. The old, walled city of Jerusalem
itself is roughly only a mile in diameter and everyone traveled by
foot or donkey, there being no streets for autos. People lived in
crowded limestone buildings with very little room for flowers or
trees; the bazaars sold the necessities, everything from lettuce to
chinaware. Our guide said Arabs here were extremely poor and
bitter about losing their land. He showed us his own house in the
Israeli sector, through the Jaffa Gate, that he was forced to leave
and could see, but never return to. And we, too, were not able to
cross over into West Jerusalem because the Arabs states would
not admit anyone who had been in Israel and we were going next
to Egypt.

We visited so many more famous sights, including the Western
Wall, or Wailing Wall, and the golden Dome of the Rock, the most
impressive landmark in the Old City. As a special favor to us, Theo
took us to the Church of the Redeemer, a Lutheran church well off
the beaten path. The latter is a fairly large church but much plainer
than most of the mosques or Catholic edifices we had seen; adorn-
ment aside, our short time there was most meaningful to Kathy and

me, *both Lutherans. I took pages of notes on the sights in the Holy Land for the long letter I planned to write to my grandfather, a Lutheran minister back in Illinois.

Afterwards, we drove up to the Mount of Olives. We climbed a small tower nearby to get a panoramic view of Jerusalem and its environs—a magnificent sight with the Judean Hills looming to the east. Our guide pointed out the route Jesus rode over to enter the city, via the Golden Gate, on Palm Sunday, and showed us several other sites of Biblical significance. We descended to the Mount of Olives and walked down to the beautiful Garden of Gethsemane at its foot, marveling at the ancient olive trees standing there, perhaps since the time of Christ. Kathy and I decided this was our favorite spot of all and we sat for a quiet time on the warm garden wall, silenced by the significance of this prayerful place.

Next we were off to Bethlehem, just five miles south, but since the partitioning of Palestine, one had to travel sixteen miles around Israel to reach the city. On the way, we saw the tomb of Rachel, the mountain where Herod lies buried, the Shepherd's Field and beyond it, the Field of Boaz, all still as the Bible described them, in settings surrounded by groves of olive trees and small fields. Then Bethlehem itself appeared, nestled on two hills south of Jerusalem. The city, then of about 10,000, was famous for its olive wood and mother-of-pearl work; I bought a crucifix made by the artisans who were employed in this craft. Since we were pressed for time, we went directly to the Church of the Nativity, the entrance to which is so low one must stoop to enter. The design kept out the mounted raiders of the past who would otherwise have ridden inside and *caused much damage.

Since everything of antiquity is now at a lower earth level, we walked down the stairs to the manger site, the Holy Grotto. Here

*because of our Luth. heritage

*ravished the treasures

again, man-made artificiality eclipsed the original simplicity of such a place—marble floors, incense burners, candles and flowers transformed the sight and disappointed me. The keepers of the shrine, the Greeks, Catholics and Armenians, seemed to be dueling for space for their adornments; still, they do preserve it and for that one should be grateful. The upper room of the church is plain and pleasant. In the church's belfry hangs the bell whose ringing one hears broadcast from Bethlehem on Christmas Eve. We left the little town singing Christmas songs at Easter time!

Touring was taking its toll and we couldn't wait to trundle off to bed so that we could get an early start the next day. We would be leaving the Holy Land, the highlight of our trip, where the Bible came alive for me, making memories I have cherished ever after. Our pilgrimage was over, still we managed to cram in several more Biblical sights before taking off in the morning bound for Cairo on a little Trans-Jordan plane that looked like it was held together with chewing gum and baling wire. We flew along the Dead Sea and over the Suez Canal, where all the bickering about the British troops was going on at the time; the rest of the scenery was sand and more sand. Finally across the desert, we landed safely and were greeted with a blast of intense heat as we deplaned.

Much to our surprise, we were met by an official from the Egyptian Ministry of State who kindly helped us get a hotel room. I must have made quite an impression when I went to the Egyptian embassy in Vienna to apply for our visas. The official there was delighted that two young American women were planning to visit his country; he asked for our itinerary and offered to help in any way to make our visit a special one. I accepted his solicitousness as mere politeness, but, obviously, it meant more than that.

We were totally beat, overwhelmed by the heat, but nonetheless accepted the Egyptian's invitation to show us around Cairo and agreed to be picked up at 5:00 p.m. We collapsed in our cool room till then. Our escort showed up at the appointed time, with a fellow government official, and drove us all around the city, past posh country club grounds, imposing buildings and museums to the waterfront where we climbed into a luxuriously outfitted felucca for a sail along the Nile. After our relaxing river ride, we went to a famous Arab restaurant where we perched on pillows to dine on delicious native food, listening all the while to the exotic music while the belly dancers executed their sinuous movements. Our new friends wanted to take us night-clubbing afterwards, but we reluctantly had to beg off, being truly exhausted. Nonetheless, it was a night to remember—my Arabian Nights fantasy made real.

Early the next day, we went to the American Express office to book a guide for our stay in Cairo. But I had another reason to go there, as well. I was hoping for, expecting, a letter from Bob to be waiting for me. And indeed it was! I was delighted, especially to read that he missed me. And I missed him, too, but was having too much fun to have given that feeling much thought. I had sent him a couple of postcards though.

Our guide was a very knowledgeable Arab who spoke English quite well. With his weather-worn face and dressed as he was in flowing gown and native head gear, he looked as if he stepped out of the pages of the Bible. Kathy was particularly obsessed with this characterization and started to refer to him as "Moses" when speaking with me. Then, one time, in her excitement at a certain scene, she slipped up and blurted out, "Oh, Moses, please take our picture here." The poor man looked quite puzzled and I couldn't stop laughing. Kathy explained her *faux pas* and our guide was

* OLD TESTAMENT

gracious enough to smile. He seemed to accept his new nickname with equanimity and so, ever after, he was Moses to us.

Moses took us to the Egyptian Museum and showed us the most important relics, mostly from King Tut's tomb, some of which dated back to 3000 B.C. We could have spent days there, but had to press on—to see the Pyramids of Giza and the Sphinx. En route, we passed the place where tradition has it the baby Moses was found in the bulrushes. We also drove by the palatial new home built for Fatima and her daughter, she the first wife of King Farouk whom he divorced because she had borne him no sons.

Then we came upon the towering pyramids. What massive, remarkable structures! I was awestruck. We were guided through the tunnels of the Pyramid of Cheops to the chamber of the king, empty, of course, but in my mind's eye full of the precious baggage that was meant to accompany the pharaoh to the next world. One of the interior guides insisted upon telling our fortunes—for a considerable fee, of course. We were certainly captive customers, stranded in a tight passageway as we were, and thus we learned that Kathy would live to the ripe old age of eighty-one and I would bear four children and have one rich son! None of this turned out to be totally true.

Upon emerging from the recesses of the pyramid, we found Moses ready for our obligatory camel ride. I held on for dear life as my camel, named "California," rose rear legs first, and off we went on a ten minute amble to see the silent Sphinx. There we dismounted and enjoyed a Coca Cola (I've saved the bottle cap with its Arabic writing) while marveling at this colossal, recumbent stone figure that stared inscrutably into space. Back on the camels again for our return walk, we found our camel escorts very chatty and very happy to accept our tips when we dismounted.

We lunched at the nearby Mena House where Roosevelt and Churchill held one of their historic meetings. The House is set amid a beautiful garden, full of palm trees and flowers; its patio was bedecked with chairs and tables sheltered by colorful umbrellas—the whole place a welcome oasis in the desert surrounding the pyramids. Before we left, I browsed in an antique shop on the premises and purchased a scarab that came with a certificate guaranteeing that it is a genuine antique dating to the twelfth dynasty, about 2600 BC. I paid fifty piasters—half an Egyptian pound—and am eligible for a refund if it is proved by any museum authority to be other than genuine. Very pleased with my purchase, I quickly decided to accept its provenance.

On our return to Cairo, Moses drove past what was once the renowned Shepherds Hotel, long since burned to the ground, and showed us the Egyptian cemeteries where cement walls are built around the family plots. We saw more mosques, one of which was singularly stunning with its hundreds of lights, turned on for about ten seconds for a tip of one dollar. We couldn't miss the bazaar, one of my favorite places wherever we traveled, and Cairo's didn't disappoint. I could not resist buying a very large, engraved brass tray—about three feet in diameter—and the intricately carved stand that would make it an ideal coffee table. Kathy succumbed as well, buying a copper tray, about two feet in diameter, but passed on the stand. Our purchases would become a huge burden to get back, but at the time we didn't give it a thought.

We stopped for the famous ice cream at Groppy's before saying goodbye to Moses at our hotel. Waiting for us there were dinner and dancing invitations from our Egyptian escorts along with gifts—silver earrings for me and a ring for Kathy. Another evening out, with a special floor show on offer as well, would have been delightful, but we were weary from sight seeing and regretfully declined. Also, we had to be up with the sun the next morning.

We hit the road at 8:00 a.m., aboard a modern bus on our way to Alexandria, a three hour drive across the sandy desert. It was like walking into an anthill, Kathy observed, as a swarm of urchins surrounded us upon arrival at the boat dock, all wanting to help as we struggled to keep track of our many pieces of baggage, including the outsize bazaar buys. The boys wanted *baksheesh*, of course. We had been plagued by this presence all across the region, but this horde was exceptional. Perhaps they knew that people might want to rid themselves of their Egyptian currency when leaving the country, as we did, but we finally had to have the police stationed at the dock intervene and ask them to leave us alone as we coped with the red tape prior to boarding our ship.

However, another delay presented itself once the paper processing was completed. I had to find a toilet. This was a request I had hesitated to make, and gamely followed the instructions I received from the customs official. I left Kathy to guard our possessions and walked a good distance away until I came to the "boardwalk" as directed. Except the boardwalk was literally just that—single planks of boards laid end to end, leading to a primitive outhouse standing alone in the sand. I had to place one foot in front of the other to avoid getting a shoe full of sand; it was like walking on a railroad track. I managed to stay balanced and eventually reached my destination. Inside, so stifling and smelly, I was confronted with a hole in the sand flanked by two indentations for one's feet. As I was straddling the hole, coping with skirt, underwear and heavy purse slung bandolier style over my chest and trying not to inhale, I pondered the plight of the male user in his ankle length garb and hoped he had as much trouble as I.

Finally aboard the *Enotria*, bound for Naples, we found our comfortable quarters and collapsed. This time our ship was a primarily a passenger vessel carrying a limited amount of cargo so the accommodations were nicer than on the *Campidoglio*. However, the weather on the Tyrrhenian Sea was nasty—cool and rainy—and we were travel-weary so, despite the added amenities, we didn't enjoy this trip nearly so much as the voyage to Athens. We were content to stay in our cabin and catch up on sleep.

Next day, we docked briefly at Syracuse, on the island of Sicily, and were guided by radar that evening through the Strait of Messina, arriving at Naples in the morning. As soon as we got ourselves situated in our hotel, we were off to Pompeii, a half an hour away by train. There we found an excellent guide who explained the fascinating ruins of the city that was destroyed by a volcano in the 1st century A.D. We were impressed at how recognizable the artifacts of that civilization were,—items such as dental instruments, a tile with the warning "beware of the dog" in Latin, hedge clippers and more. There is really nothing new under the sun. The people had bathhouses with lead pipes for running water, houses with atria, and several surviving objects demonstrated their unabashed view of sexuality. Very graphically!

As an eleven year old, I had read with great relish about Pompeii in Richard Halliburton's marvelous *Book of Marvels, The Occident*. The book was a birthday present from my dear aunts who lived in Los Angeles. That city itself seemed a world away from my midwestern home and, in the pages of the book, there were wonders of an even wider world, so temptingly described, beckoning to me. Like the author, I wished "my father, or somebody, would take me to all these wonderful places." And he did! To mark our graduations—I from college and my sister from high school—daddy drove our family to the Deepest Canyon, the Greatest Dam, San Francisco and the Golden Gate Bridge, and at last to Los Angles to see those very aunts whose gift had whetted my appetite for adventure. Now I was seeing many more of Halliburton's sights for myself—St. Peter's, the Blue Grotto, Santa Sophia, the Acropolis, Athena's Temple. Later travels would take me to see the Kremlin, St. Basil's Cathedral, Gibraltar, Mount St. Michael.

The next stop on my Halliburton-like trail was the Isle of Capri, a two hour ride by boat from Naples. When the boat reached the mouth of the Blue Grotto, we transferred to a rowboat and had to sit on its bottom so we could slip through the small opening in the mountainside that led into the enchanted cave. It was a sunny day and on such a day the sunlight on the sea outside penetrates the cavern through a submerged opening, then flows up through the water inside, to shine upon the walls. The influx causes the water inside to appear a beautiful fluorescent aquamarine and when we looked back toward the entrance, we were captivated by the sight of the unearthly blue light dancing on the walls of the grotto! The effect reminded Kathy of dropping bluing into a laundry tub of rinse water, only on a much larger scale. An earthy description, but apt. I simply thought it was magical.

That impression extended to Capri itself; the whole island was a fairyland aerie. We were taken high up on the island to a charming hotel for lunch; the view was dazzling. We went even farther up to see King Farouk's mansion and strolled around in the enchanting gardens and did a bit of shopping. Finally, we took a chair lift all the way to the top of the mountain. We felt like we were sitting on top of the world, with seas and cities at our feet.

But we had to come down, literally and figuratively, and rush back to Naples. On the return boat ride, I felt the urge to break into song—

and did. Inspired, I serenaded my companions with "Santa Lucia," "Funiculi, Funicula," and some other songs not even Italian. Once on dry land, we dashed to the station to catch the train to Rome. We were dead tired and slept the entire two hour trip—sitting up. By midnight, we were sleeping soundly in the beds at our hotel.

We awoke to discover Rome, the Eternal City. It is magnificent. Full of history, friendly though frantic. And offering fabulous food. I loved the salads and veal scallopini. We had fettucini Alfredo at Alfredo's and pizza, the original kind, at an outdoor café. As we left the place, I walked close by another table where a couple of handsome Italian men were enjoying drinks and was greeted with a friendly pinch on my bottom as I passed. I was startled, but took it as a compliment and later learned that's how the gesture is meant.

We took a conducted tour to see all the sights: the massive St. Peter's Cathedral in the Vatican and the awe-inspiring Michelangelo frescoes on the ceiling and the altar wall of the Sistine Chapel, completed when he was actually working as a sculptor, not a painter; the Catacombs; the ruins of the ancient Colosseum; the Pantheon and the Holy Staircase in the cathedral of St. John of the Lateran.

I strolled alone through the incomparable Villa Borghese grounds, delighting in the romantic island set in a little lake in the park. I saw the balcony from which Mussolini delivered his public addresses, the striking Viktor Emmanuel monument nearby, the Spanish steps and later joined Kathy for a little window shopping, which was all we could afford at this stage. The shops displayed beautiful clothing and I noticed how well dressed the people were despite what seemed to me to be rather high prices.

The day before we were to leave for Vienna, I had an audience with the Pope, one of the many to crowd inside the Vatican. With ticket in hand, plus a rosary Kathy had bought for her boss and a crucifix purchased for our landlady, both of which she wanted blessed, I presented myself at "10:00 a.m. precise" at the *Portone di Bronzo*. I was ushered into a large, imposing chamber where Pope Pius XII appeared, in glorious dress, to dispense a papal benediction. As a confirmed Lutheran, I had been most curious about Catholic rituals and found this a very impressive ceremony. As we filed out, believers were able to kiss the Pope's ring. When it came my turn in line, I merely bowed my head yet the Pope spoke the same words to me as he had to his faithful. I felt as blessed as the artifacts in my hand.

Kathy had not gone with me. She was off to Monte Carlo to meet up with the Navy man she had gotten reacquainted with in Istanbul. I was happy that she was making this side excursion, but she left me with an enormous load of baggage—both huge trays, my tray stand, all our other purchases, and two suitcases. Thank goodness my hotel was close to the station. Somehow, with the help of a porter from the hotel, I managed to stagger to the station and cram everything into the sleeper compartment on the train to Venice. However, at 6:30 in the morning, I had to move into a day coach and lug all the *Pack und Sack* through several cars to my seat. The train crossed the border into Austria at 11:20 a.m. and by 9:40 that night it chugged into Vienna's South Station. How wonderful it was to see Bob waiting for me. The next day, we met Kathy's train.

My Middle East odyssey was a stellar experience—exciting, enlightening, enriching—and fun. I saw so much of the world, met so many of its people and learned a lot. I realized how fortunate I was to have had that opportunity and returned to work refreshed, if not rested. Everybody seemed pleased to see me again so I felt confident there were no lingering ill feelings that may have been aroused by my departing behavior. I jumped back into work eagerly and energetically.

Some time later, I ran into the chief of operations in the hall.

"How was your trip, Shirley?" Bill inquired.

"Just wonderful, thanks," I replied. "But it's good to be back."

"You know, Peter had put in for a promotion for you, but asked me to withdraw it after he heard of your refusing to finish that copying job before you left."

I was stunned and so very disappointed. Now I would have to prove myself all over again. Would I have acted as I did if I had known I was up for a promotion? Probably not. So, I guess I got what I deserved, and learned a hard lesson. When my boss resubmitted the promotion request some months later and after it finally came through, I felt I not only had earned it but also had paid for it in full.

WEDDING DAY

Autumn arrived—a beautiful season in Vienna. For a while, the Wiener Wald was decked out in its fall finery but by the end of October, the leaves had deserted the trees. All Hallows Eve was around the corner. For us, it meant Halloween was approaching. Bob and I were invited to a costume party and I began to wonder what to wear. Everyone would be renting costumes usually worn to *Fasching* events; I was hoping to appear in something more original—but what?

Then, one day as I was flipping through a fashion magazine, I found the answer. A daring new ad campaign by Maidenform showed women in all kinds of business and social situations wearing elegant outfits—but just their Maidenform bras on top! The tag lines read, "I dreamed I went to the opera—or to a business meeting, etc.—in my Maidenform Bra." Thus inspired, I dreamed I went to a Halloween party in my Maidenform Bra—and did! My costume was completed with a black evening skirt, a white stole, pearls, and featured my lacy white bra that was indeed by Maidenform! Bob highly approved. We both had a great time.

One evening later that year, Bob and I were out to dinner at the Beethoven House and between the soup course and the entrée, he proposed! I gulped down a swallow of wine I had just sipped and said unhesitatingly, "Yes!" We managed a celebratory, and tasty, kiss before the meat course arrived. Soon we were making plans to get married. Bob was in the CIC but he had to be cleared by the CIA before we could do so. Also, we found out the Army had to clear me despite my top secret clearance from the CIA. We didn't know how long these processes would take, but aimed for a wedding date in early March.

We celebrated our engagement twice. Once, with a group of friends at the *Weinschenke zum Dritten Mann* and later, around Christmas time, at a party at my apartment in the Skodagasse. A keepsake from that memorable evening out is an autographed post-card showing Anton Karas, the musician of "The Third Man" theme fame, at the zither accompanied by his two accordionists. The ensemble serenaded us with special music to mark our special event, making that souvenir all the more meaningful.

Soon, however, our plans hit a snag. I suffered from chronic sore throat, exacerbated, I'm sure, by the damp winters of Wien. Once, when I was completely miserable, I had to go to the Army hospital for relief and was diagnosed with tonsillitis. Bob declared that I should have my tonsils out before we got married. It seemed that he was as much affected by my repeated illnesses as I was. Eventually, I saw the wisdom of having a tonsillectomy although I had heard gruesome tales of its effects on adults. Nonetheless, I bravely made arrangements and ventured one January morning to the hospital buoyed up by the prospect of being free of sore throats forever.

The Austrian doctor directed me to a straight-backed chair in an examining room. I sat down and he handed me a kidney shaped pan.

"Excuse me, but what is this for?"

"It's a drip pan," the doctor explained in excellent English, "you hold it up to your mouth to catch your tonsils in."

Before I could protest, the doctor was swabbing my throat with some numbing solution. Then he approached with a needle that looked a foot long. He pried open my mouth as wide as it would go and injected the local anesthetic in the tonsil area. When I was numb and couldn't talk and scarcely could breathe, he proceeded to cut. I was gagging and spitting blood and holding onto the pan all the while worrying if I would ever be able to sing again, let alone speak! After this brutal but blessedly brief experience, I was led to a woman's ward and put to bed.

The nurse disappeared after announcing she would bring me something to drink. I could hardly swallow because it was so painful; how could I manage to drink anything? I lay there wondering why I had ever consented to this operation. After a long time, a nurse's aide appeared with cup of HOT tea! Now not only was I miserable, I was furious—and couldn't say a thing. Bob came to visit after work, bearing a beautiful bouquet and a carton of ice cream. He put a bit on my tongue; I let it melt away, soothing my sore, sore throat.

That night was a nightmare. There were forty beds on the ward, and forty patients. One woman was hallucinating, I was sure. Her screams were terrible and roused the rest of us. She was led away, poor thing, and people tried to get back to sleep. I was not successful and was determined to leave the next day, which I did, well or not. My landlady mothered me, making "snow pudding" that slid down so smoothly, and soon brought me back to health.

Now wedding plans could progress. I asked my boss, Peter, to walk me down the aisle since my parents couldn't travel to our wedding. He happily agreed, but then turned up with his leg in a cast and begged off. I wondered how it had happened, but, preoccupied with wedding plans, asked another surrogate to play "father of the bride." All of a sudden my boss became extremely concerned about our wedding date. It seems the date we chose was right in the middle of an extremely active spy season—several Soviet defections and security restrictions had everyone on the alert and on guard, especially the Soviets.

Nonetheless, Bob and I brightened a gloomy day in March as we were married in the small Lutheran Church in the Dorothegasse and just about everybody from both our offices attended. Our reception was at the Hotel Sacher. I had to convince the hotel management that, for my wedding cake, I did not want the traditional chocolate *Sacher Torte*, for which the hotel was so famous, but rather, a white cake. I held my breath as we cut into the beautiful confection and was relieved to see it was indeed white.

We had finally gotten permission from the station chief to travel through the Soviet zone on our honeymoon but only if we were locked in the courier compartment of the Mozart with a military guard stationed outside the door! Our orders were to leave the train station as inconspicuously as possible. Here were two people actively involved in operations against the Soviets—what a catch we would be!

So, the morning after our wedding, we rose at dawn and arrived at the *Bahnhof*, all dark and quiet, and waited on the empty platform for the train. Suddenly, we heard a loud noise—a loud musical noise—in fact, an oompah band was marching toward us followed by just about everybody from both of our offices who had been at the wedding! And they were shouting, singing and generally making such a racket we were convinced all Vienna was aware of our departure. The Mozart pulled up in the midst of this bedlam and we were escorted aboard amid a shower of rice and confetti. What a send-off! Security be damned!

Friends were driving our car through the zone and we waited and waited at the Enns checkpoint for them. Hours went by. I had visions of their being held by the Soviets, as I had been. But finally they arrived—they'd had a flat tire, that's all. So at last we were off to the Italian Riviera—away from damp, gray, spook-filled Vienna.

Upon my return, I learned that my boss's leg had not been broken, that the cast had been a ruse to lure a potential defector to his home. It worked, and the Russian was put on a special plane and flown out of the city "black," that is, without any clearance from or notice to the Austrian airfield authorities. No one was to tell me before the honeymoon so that it would be one less thing I'd know, in case something were to happen to me!

So off we had gone, blissfully unaware of the real reason for the restrictions.

Much, much later I learned that even that explanation was a fiction and perhaps it was fashioned because of me—to give my boss a plausible excuse for not being in my wedding without having to disclose the real reason. There really were a number of defections at that time, one in particular happened in mid-February, just two weeks before our wedding. But this man was a walk-in, not an induced defector. He was Peter Deriabin, a KGB officer, possibly the most valuable intelligence defector since the war, according to Bill Hood, the chief of operations at the Vienna station. And, the defector wasn't flown out of Vienna. He was smuggled out of the city in the baggage car of the Mozart, cleverly encased in an old hot water tank discarded by the CIC whose personnel also helped craft the camouflage.*

As Hood recalled, when he and Peter arrived at the train station with their precious cargo, they found it crawling with Soviet surveillance types but managed to board without incident. The trip was nerve-racking for them and the man in the tank, for the Soviets could have stopped the train and searched it. But they and their secret passenger made it safely through the checkpoint. Given the high alert surrounding all this espionage activity, the station obviously had to assume that the Soviets would continue their surveillance for a while and they were right to be concerned

---

*Ibid, pp. 159-162.

about the safety of the Perrys traveling through the Soviet zone and any secrets we might have. Clearly, we did not have the need to know beforehand.

Deriabin turned out to be the deputy chief of security for the Soviet colony in Vienna. As such, he was able to confirm to us, through circuitous questioning, that Popov was not a suspect in the eyes of Soviet security. He also provided a roster of the KGB in Vienna.*

So, not only did we now know that Popov was clean, we had detailed information that confirmed what we, in our Soviet section, had already collected and what Popov had given us.* The Soviets' loss was certainly our gain.

---

*Ibid, pp. 164-165.

AT HOME

The Perrys settled into a comfortable, one-bedroom apartment in the city's tallest building at the time; it was known as the *Hochhaus* and was fourteen stories high. It was nicely furnished and had a fully functioning kitchen, but I didn't spend much time there because we had a cleaning woman who also liked to cook. One day when I came home from work, she was still there and called out to me in an excited voice, in English, that she had made an awful pee! I was aghast and called back anxiously, "Where?"

"In der küche, natürlich," she replied in German.

Ok, naturally, in the kitchen, thought I, where else would one make an awful pee! I rushed into the kitchen and scanned the floor—no mess there at all, thanks be. Then I noticed her standing by the table in the corner pointing proudly to—an apple pie! Perhaps she had wanted to say "apple" but pronounced it more like the German *Apfel* so that I heard her wrong and thought she said "awful." And, in German, the diphthong "ie" is pronounced like the second vowel, so "pie" would be "pee" in a literal translation. Anyway, I was greatly relieved to see the pie, and to discover later what a delicious dessert it was.

THE TAIL

My working world was getting ever more interesting. Often reports written by my husband crossed my desk but, of course, I never told him that. I kept the Soviet mug book up to date; I wrote reports to headquarters. Then one day, I was assigned to do surveillance. My first such experience was one I shall never forget.

I was in position in an apartment in a safe house one floor above the apartment where a case officer was meeting with his Russian agent. A safe house was a house or apartment the CIA rented in the American sector of Vienna that was a relatively secure place to meet an agent; it would have been swept for bugs and its location monitored to make sure it was unknown to the opposition. But we changed these places regularly, never being quite sure how safe they really were.

I was listening in on the conversation below with huge headphones hugging my ears. I had to know the minute the meeting was over so I could leave in time to follow the agent. The apartment was unheated, but this was fortunate—I could keep my coat on, my Austrian loden coat, as well as the scarf I had tied over my head—and sit there, anxious and ready to run. I strained to hear the voices. They were speaking Russian, a language I didn't know so I had to intuit when the talking was winding down.

At last I heard the door below bang shut. I yanked off the headphones and grabbed my things and bolted up. But now that the time had come, I found that I could not walk! I had to get down three flights of stairs and pick up the guy, and my legs had gone completely limp, so tensed up was I. On my knees, I crawled to the door and fell out into the hall. My heart was pounding. I grabbed the banister and tugged myself upright. Hand over hand, hanging onto the banister as I bounced down on my butt, I propelled myself along. At the top of the last flight of stairs, my legs began to feel alive again. I could stand up. Holding on to the banister, I managed to stumble down the rest of the way and after what seemed like an eternity, making noise I was sure resounded throughout the building, I reached the front door. Fortunately, my legs had regained most of their function and I tried to regain some measure of composure before bursting out onto the street.

I looked around frantically for my quarry—so much for appearing nonchalant! My job was to see if anyone was following him, because, if so, it would mean the KGB suspected the man and the whole operation would then be at risk. We also wanted to know where he went after the meeting and would have a tail on him all the way to his return destination. I spotted him ambling down the street. Thank goodness he wasn't moving very fast and hadn't gotten very far.

I crossed to the other side of the street the better to keep him in view. We knew the agent's regular route to the streetcar stop and I prayed he wouldn't deviate from it. Thanks be, he didn't. A case officer would be waiting at the streetcar stop to follow the agent home. When I arrived at the stop for the hand-off, I was to stand by the signpost as if consulting the route information posted there. If all was secure, I was to indicate it by holding in my left hand my *Einkaufsnet* (a mesh sack all the good *Hausfrauen* used to carry their grocery purchases), which I did. I had made sure my bag had some produce sticking out of it—leeks and celery served the purpose well. If anything had gone wrong, the sack would be in my right hand and the case officer would decide his next step. He would be watching me but I was not to make eye contact with him. After a reasonable time, when I felt certain my colleague had determined the signal, I was to stand back and appear to be waiting for another streetcar, presumably one leaving after the agent and his new tail had departed. I did everything right and everything worked out OK, much to my great relief, but I had learned well what the phrase "weak in the knees" means!

NEW YEAR'S EVE

So quickly, it seemed, my two-year tour of duty, plus a few months, was up as was my husband's. Bob and I were to leave Europe the Army way. He the military man, and I, the dependent. We were to sail from Livorno (Leghorn), Italy, a few days after Christmas, 1954, but first we had to deliver our car to the Army docks there so it could be shipped back to the States.

We were in a happy, holiday-like mood, looking forward to our return to the States and our last trip in Europe. We set out in our sporty MG-TD convertible with the top up and the side curtains as secure as we could make them. The car's British racing green paint shone brilliantly in the early December sun as we left Vienna. On the way to the port, we were planning a short detour to Milan to visit the Borsalino hat factory there. Our itinerary would take us first to Innsbruck and then south, through the Tyrolean Alps via the Brenner Pass, to Italy. This route was the only way over the Alps long before the modern highway was built.

Late in the day we reached the border and as we climbed the mountain, under 5000 feet but seemingly high as the heavens, we encountered some fog. We hoped it wouldn't last for the length of the pass—some fifty-nine miles. But the fog did not lift, instead, it became thicker, so dense, in fact that neither of us could even see the road ahead. And now it was night. Bob was driving blind.

We were creeping along, ever upward, Bob squinting intently ahead and I trying to see the side of the road through the celluloid side curtains. All was opaque; we could see nothing. How would we ever make it over the Pass at this rate, I wondered. Suddenly, the car ground to a stop.

My heart skipped a beat; I wanted to shout a warning at Bob but tried to sound matter-of-fact, "There's no shoulder, Bob, don't try to pull over."

"I know," he said. His voice was tense. He gave me a worried look; I couldn't tell if he was as scared as I. I think he was but he had a plan.

"We can't go on like this, Shirl. You'll have to get out and walk alongside the car and guide me. It's the only way we'll be able to move."

"You're right," I gulped. I hesitated for only a moment, then yanked the side curtain out of its slots, so we could communicate, and got out. Not only was there no shoulder, there was no guard rail either, and now I was cold to boot. I inched my foot ahead to see how close the car was to the edge of the road. We were right at the edge! There was just enough room for me to walk alongside. It's just as well that I couldn't see over the edge—where the abyss awaited.

We began to roll again, no faster than I could walk. I positioned myself opposite the right front fender and as my foot felt its way along, I would call back, "The road is curving, bear a little left," or "Stay straight." Sometimes I went a step or two ahead, to get a feel for the direction, but really couldn't foretell much. Once my foot slipped over the edge and I went down on my knees. I was frantic but fortunately the car had moved forward enough so I could grab the door and pull myself up. That was a close call.

Bob was shouting, "Are you all right?" I was, thank God.

But this was an agonizing experience for the both of us. I dared not let myself think how long it would go on. Time had evaporated. I'd been walking for what seemed hours. Surely, it wasn't. I wanted to ask Bob how far he thought we had progressed but didn't want to distract him. I worried and wondered how he was doing while I struggled along.

Finally, my fright and fatigue caught up with me. I dropped back to the windowless door and hollered inside, "Bob, I just don't think I can go any farther." Our situation seemed hopeless. I couldn't think of a saving solution but knew my guidance afoot wasn't it.

Then, just at that very minute, when I had reached the depths of discouragement, Bob shouted back, "Shirl, get in, get in! I can see specks of light in the rear view mirror. It has to be headlights! Get in! We're going to follow him."

It was indeed headlights! A car was coming! It was providential! I scrambled into the car. We idled a moment, waiting for the auto to approach and pass us. I could scarcely breathe; Bob gripped his hands on the steering wheel, bracing himself for some white knuckle driving. The car roared past, hugging the mountain side, then swerved in front of us and raced on. The MG sprang to life, hot on its tail. What a fool that driver was, I thought, hurtling along this unmarked mountain road. But it was a road he must have known well and, trusting his familiarity with the route, we hurtled after him.

"Gotta keep his tail lights in view," Bob shouted, pressing on the accelerator. We flew through the thick fog, careening around the curves, focused on the little red lights, our passage out of the Pass. The wind blew in, cold and bracing. The tissues in the box on the tunnel waved back and forth. My teeth began to chatter. All the while, Bob's skill at the wheel kept us close behind the little Fiat 500 *Topolino*.

He allowed himself an observation out loud while still staring straight ahead, "I didn't know that little mouse could go so fast."

We laughed a nervous little laugh. The *Topolino*, its name does mean "little mouse," was one of the smallest cars in the world at the time, a real micro machine, but it could go like stink. Actually, we were going only about fifty miles an hour but it felt like we were speeding along at one hundred!

I panicked when the tail lights would disappear, when the *Topolino* took a curve in the road, but Bob bravely barreled on, as if he could see a red vapor trail through the fog, showing the way. At last, it seemed we were descending. Please, let it be so, I silently prayed. Yes, we were really heading down! The fog was fading! We could see the road!

We slowed down. The little mouse had disappeared for good but we were safe and sound in Italy.

We stopped at the first *Gasthaus* we came to. We didn't know for sure where we were, but it didn't matter. We struggled up to a room with our luggage and fell into bed. No thought of eating, which was fortunate because in a little while I had to run down the hall to the WC where I lost whatever was in my upset stomach. The hair-raising walk alongside the car, the wild ride down the mountain, the whole treacherous trip finally had its effect on me, but now the nightmare was over. Bob slept soundly; I finally got some rest. The next morning, I felt fine and so did Bob.

Our visit to the Borsalino factory in Milan cheered us both. Coming away with two beautiful felts, which later became two fashionable hats, erased all my former fears and Bob was delighted with his bowler. Later, with the car safely delivered to the docks, we boarded a train for our return to Vienna, which was, happily, an uneventful trip.

Soon after, we were at sea, celebrating New Year's Eve in the middle of the Mediterranean. The Sea, known for its turbulence, especially in winter, was extremely unsettled and a big, bad storm hit just as we all assembled for a special holiday dinner. Tables, chairs, glass and china crashed around as the ship, an old Liberty bottom from WWII days, pitched up and down. We all fell from our seats and slid back and forth on the floor, covered in food and drink, cut from the broken glass and black and blue from banging into the walls and each other. What a way to welcome a new year!

Aboard ship, we wives were separated from our spouses, the military men going to their quarters and the dependents to theirs. As a dependent without children, I was lowest on the berthing pole. In fact, I was assigned to E deck, two decks below the water line, next to the hold. The bad thing was that there were so many women with children aboard that my cell-like cabin also housed two wives with "one each baby," according to military speak. The other wife and cell mate was pregnant, so we two drew the upper berths. Actually, that turned out to be a good thing because I could climb above the clotheslines hung with diapers and stockings and assorted underwear and try to blot out the sounds of crying babies, the expectant mother throwing up, the rattle of baby food jars being washed in the one and only sink and the unceasing chatter.

My escape, once I was above the fray, was to read. I plowed through all of Joyce's *Ulysses*—a demanding choice, but it certainly kept my mind off my surroundings. I managed to fend off seasickness, however I almost threw up reading about the delicacies Mr. Leopold Bloom savored—such awful offal! My innards quivered just visualizing his eating "with relish" those "inner organs of beasts and fowls." Urp! But I was tantalized by Molly's soliloquy, amazed at all her cheating ways—so all in all, the book certainly served the purpose of distracting me. The distraction aside, I did feel so sorry for my bunkmates, those poor women having to cope with their babies in our cramped quarters. At the same time, I was most unhappy at my own sorry state, for I became constipated and remained so for the entire three weeks of the voyage!

My husband would smuggle out a breakfast orange from his early seating, because, at my seating, the third and last, there was nothing left to eat but bread, stale at that. We had remains for dinner, too. He surreptitiously passed the orange to me when we met each afternoon for four hours, our only time together. We couldn't go out on deck because of the bad weather so during this interval we sat inside, rocking and rolling with the churning sea, and played gin rummy, non-stop, running up thousands of points.

During that storm on New Year's Eve, the ship lost its port stabilizer and slowed down to a crawl. We put in at the Azores for repairs but whatever was done didn't bring us back up to speed and necessitated our traveling at half speed all the way across the North Atlantic. Since the top speed of these Liberty ships was eleven knots, it's no wonder why the crossing took three weeks. We encountered a couple more storms and survived more tossings about en route and finally limped into the Brooklyn Navy Yard in the dead cold January of a New York winter.

My three week ordeal had rendered me bloated and sallow-faced. I worried terribly about what to do with my lackluster hair in preparation for disembarking, finally opting to hide it with a scarf tied, babushka style, under my chin. I had on my warm loden coat and Austrian boots and big bulky mittens and carried a bulging tote bag. I looked for all the world like a war bride or, worse, a refugee. And I was about to meet my in-laws for the first time! To make matters worse, I would be clomping down the gangplank with my husband who looked resplendent in his neatly pressed uniform, trim coat and shiny shoes with nothing hanging on his arm but me.

His parents spotted us right away and I remember being so nervous, not knowing what to call them, afraid I wouldn't make a good first impression. But then, as we approached them, I saw my mother-in-law look at me sympathetically and heard her say, "Oh, you poor dear" and I thought everything would be all right—until I realized she was addressing her son, not me!

UNDER THE WIRE

Back in Washington, I received a promotion to case officer status and was slated to undertake extensive training at a domestic operations base somewhere in Virginia. I would be down at the Farm, as the place was called. Case officers were required to attend this special school in order to qualify for assignments of increased responsibility and I was quite pleased to be selected to go—not everyone was. So I was determined to do well, although I had no idea of all that was involved.

I remember so much of that unique experience very clearly. I remember setting out for the site, a long, hot car ride from Washington, D.C., and the military look of the place—the dusty parade ground, bordered by nondescript barracks set in exact alignment, the precisely marked parking area—all colorless and impersonal. In fact, it was an old military base and a military atmosphere prevailed, but this didn't intimidate me—rather it intrigued me. I had always wondered what it would be like to be "in the Army," to be subject to regulations that ruled one's life, to have little choice in daily decisions, and, on a very domestic level, to be relieved of shopping, cooking, laundry, and so on.

Indeed, I got a little taste of the military life. Women and men stayed in separate barracks; we wore fatigues, ate in a mess and abided by a curfew. We were also exercised, hiked and given survival training. However, the greatest part or our time was spent in classrooms—bare, hard-benched barracks rooms that were unbearably hot and stuffy. Small windows brought in the dry summer air that was circulated in a narrow swath by a noisy floor fan. The instructor, in wilted khaki, squeaked his chalk on the blackboard to emphasize a country's GNP or list its Communist leaders. Everyone sat up straight, and sweated. But I, academic achiever that I was, reveled in it all, and learned a lot.

We were there to learn—all about the geographic area that corresponded to our particular desk assignment; for example, if one were on the Polish desk, one would be immersed in everything Polish. Area knowledge, including the military, economic, political, and cultural facts, was important for every desk officer. One could not target intelligence-gathering efforts nor evaluate what was collected without such background information. This school gave us a crash course in area knowledge.

Most of us were serious about the training. I certainly was. I remember feeling so empowered, so important, yet rather overwhelmed that I was entrusted with so much responsibility implied by my attendance there. However, my dedication, and that of the others, didn't prevent us from enjoying the strategically scheduled "happy hours." Like other professionals who deal with life and death issues on a daily basis, we welcomed the respite. I can still hear Jack playing the old upright in the so-called officers' club where we all would hang out after sessions. Jack was good. I would sing along.

"You sound pretty good, Shirley," he allowed, "but I wish you could remember the words."

I never could remember all the words, but the happy hour crowd would join in and provide them. There was an easy camaraderie; esprit was high. As for any group assembled for special assignments, our off-hours provided release from concerns about the weighty work we were being prepared to do.

The days went by routinely. We would go home over the weekends and return, ready to tackle whatever the next classes offered. We were soon quite accepting of the regimen, as, I suppose, the successful soldier becomes during his basic training. We concentrated on our area studies and tradecraft and tried to get enough sleep. More and more, the focus of our lectures honed in on the realities of the intelligence mission: how to get the information the decision-makers needed. There was only one possible way back then: from people who could find out and inform us. This meant recruiting agents in place or sending agents back into the satellite countries from which they had escaped. We were to concentrate on the latter.

Of course, thorough vetting took place before anyone was considered cleared for "going back in" but we were not overly concerned with that phase of operations at the Farm. As part of the course, we were to become intimately familiar with the reasons and risks of sending an agent across a border—black. Such an entry was far different from the dispatch of an agent well documented with false papers and a cover story—which was indeed done. Rather, it was the kind of quick and dirty entry by which an agent crossed through the no-man's border land and, in a few hours, if all went well, was back in Hungary or Czechoslovakia as himself! So that we case officers would know just what we were asking these border-crossers to do, we were to experience for ourselves just what they would go through. We were going to cross a simulated border! Mine would be the Czech border.

The prospect of convincing anyone to do just that seemed almost impossible to me yet I knew dedicated anti-Communists did return by this means. I also knew that not everyone made it.

These human resources were vital, and selecting, preparing and sending them over had to be justified by overriding intelligence requirements and a full assessment of the risks involved. So that we would know just what we were asking an agent to do, we were going to experience just what he would go through. We were going in—black—in a simulated border crossing. I was excited at the thought of it, exhilarated really. What a challenge it would be!

As I studied the Czech border (Czechoslovakia was my desk assignment), it came to me that this was very serious business. In our mock crossings, we could be caught in the searchlights, shot at (with blanks) or discovered by the dog patrols. We might encounter guards who would arrest us or stumble on land mines that would explode as flares. Only if we arrived in the woods far on the other side of the border area would we have made it across successfully. Sobering prospects all.

The borders were set up to simulate exactly each country's real border, down to the intervals between a search light sweep and the condition of the terrain. We were told we could cross anytime during the last week of training. Everyone tensed up, contemplated the weather (we had no radios or newspapers), and made his go or no-go decision based on best estimates of conditions particular to the borders involved.

I waited and worried. I prayed for rain because my plan was to dig under the fence and ground softened by rain would make the task easier. Rain could also camouflage my scent from the guard dogs. But rain could also make a quagmire of the border stretch, which was plowed ground. On balance, I decided rain would be my friend and kept praying. I was also waiting for the moon to wane for I didn't want to be caught in the moonlight either. The end of the week seemed a propitious time.

Meanwhile, results of early crossers circulated.

"Mercedes was mowed down," Bill reported.

"I heard the dogs got Ted," I volunteered.

It seemed no one had yet made it into the safe haven of the woods, or at least the grapevine hadn't picked up such news for as soon as each student finished this final test, he left camp and no announcement was made about the outcome. Our numbers dwindled steadily. Did so-and-so actually get through, we wondered? It was eerily real because a case officer who awaited word about an actual operation wouldn't be sure for a long while and worries would mount.

Finally, I could delay no longer. Time was running out and I remember feeling that I couldn't have taken the tension one day more. Late on Friday afternoon, I set out determined to make my move that night, no matter what. I was cheered by a light drizzle that had started in the morning. Maybe I wouldn't even need the small shovel I had with me, which I would leave at the fence in any event.

I ate a candy bar and hid in the friendly scrub till the cloudy darkness came, observing the guard post activities and stationing myself at a mid-point between two of them. The comings and goings of the searchlight and the patrol was exactly as had been described. Would some extraneous event cause the timings to change? It was always possible. I could only hope not. Everything seemed so crystal clear in my head—it will work, I can do this, I was sure!

I edged out of the sheltering brush on my stomach, slithering ever closer to the fence. Its barbs seemed to twinkle in the dim light, teasing me on. The ground was harder than I had anticipated. I pulled myself along until I reached a fence post around which the earth seemed softer. I started to dig. The shovel almost hit the post and the wire and could have made noise enough to attract attention, so I used my hands. Slowly, awkwardly, I scooped out the clingy clay, pushing it to the side. The rain started in earnest, which actually helped, but I could scarcely see, and my nose began to run. I had smeared my face with mud, but now I was covered with it. I felt as if I were suffocating and gulped for breath. My legs started to tremble and I lost track of the timing interval until a sweep of light scared me back to my senses—partially.

I remember feeling as if I had been digging forever and knew I had to try to get under the wire so that I could scoop out some earth ahead of me and wiggle through. I pushed myself down in the hole, barely deep enough and, lying there, partly under the fence, reached ahead, moving clay out of the way of my face, inching myself forward all the while. I realized I couldn't do this for the length of me—5'7"—and would have to turn over and sit up at some point. Suddenly my limbs seemed lame, disconnected from my torso. I couldn't move and couldn't tell how far through I was.

When was the patrol due? A beam of light again helped me rally. Somehow I flipped over and saw my legs still captive. I sat up and pulled each one from under the fence. I remember the fright that now set in. I couldn't think. I was soaked and scared and couldn't see. My mouth was dry and I gladly gulped the rainwater falling steadily now. All I knew was that there were about sixty yards of choppy ground between safety and me. I had planned to run crouched over, but when I stood up, my legs buckled. I crawled then, flopping down flat once again when the light swept over me. No alarm went off! Thank God. I was OK, but mired in mud.

"I've got to finish, got to make it," the mantras of the training kicked in and I crawled some more, trying to think when the next sweep would come. I could hear muffled voices from the patrol along the perimeter of the fence. Should I lie low or try to make a run for it? Before I could decide, it was quiet again; the patrol had passed me by! I got up to run, bending over, and stumbled, falling face first in the mud. More lights, more blessed rain drowning out my sounds and, I hoped, masking me in the darkness. At last I could see the trees ahead. I was almost there! I stood up but could not run, I had no strength in my legs, my feet felt heavy as lead weighted down as they were with mud. Only sheer will impelled me on, half crawling, half crouching, for what seemed a lifetime. I cried out as I tripped over a root and rolled into the woods! I had done it!

The exhilaration was as intense as my fear had been. I wanted to shout and cry at the same time. I was alive with nervous energy but collapsed at the base of a big oak tree, feeling completely protected from the elements—and from the enemy. The rescue team found me and showered me with congratulations. They whisked me back to camp for a bath and a beer. Later, back at my desk at headquarters, I recall thinking I would never lightly propose to dispatch a border-crosser under the wire. I had learned the lesson of this exercise well.

Ever since that experience, so riveted in my mind, I have held in high regard the Cold War warriors who went back in. Unsung heroes, these, who risked their lives for all of us in the West in the hopes of eventually improving their own lots. And for all our training and simulated experiences, we agency officers could only begin to fathom the extent of their fears and their risks, their bravery when pursuing their missions for us in that real world during the cold, Cold War.

Years later, the CIA switched to high technology intelligence gathering, abandoning, for the most part, the use of human resources that had always been the best intelligence sources—and the bravest.

This policy, I hear, has been re-evaluated, for there is no substitute for HUMINT (human intelligence) in the espionage business.

2

Dog Days

*Dogs give continuity to one's life;
they help hold the fractured pieces of it together.*
—Willie Morris

MORO, ILLINOIS

*T*he minute my aunt and uncle drove up in front of our house, I ran out to welcome them. It was always exciting to have company, especially Aunt Kitty and Uncle Tommy who lived close by and came over often. My aunt almost always brought something along to eat for dinner or for the picnics we planned. Maybe she'd have deviled eggs or one of her pecan pies! But this time she was empty-handed. My minor disappointment, however, was quickly offset by my uncle's announcement that he had something for me. He reached into his jacket pocket and pulled out what looked like a furry ball! It fit in the palm of his hand.

"What on earth is that, Uncle Tommy?"

"Here, you hold it," he replied, placing the tiny shape in my hand. It moved! It raised its head and stretched out its little paws. It was a puppy!

"For me?"

"Well, for the family, if your mother agrees."

What could she say? I was already smitten with the little animal and immediately named him "Fuzzy"—it described him exactly. He grew to have long brown and white hair, a long white tail, stand-up ears and a pointed snout—I'd swear that he could smile.

Thus began my devotion to dogs. I had no recollection of Arno, the German Shepherd that Mother and Dad had when I was born, for he was shipped off to a vineyard after biting a neighbor boy who came into our yard where I was sitting in a stroller, guarded, as always, by the faithful Shepherd. No doubt the dog mistook the boy's friendly approach for a threat to me, for Arno considered me his charge, a small creature to be defended from all untoward advances.

Fuzzy, a mixture of Spitz and terrier, was small and feisty. But he was exceptionally tolerant when my sister and I would dress him up and parade him around in a doll buggy. He was a member of the family and I loved him. I wrote odes to him and stories about him; I called him "little stout heart." Fuzzy would take on all comers and got into many a dogfight, usually at his instigation. Once he was brought home on a towel, virtually in pieces after a vicious go-around with a dog several times his size and Mother miraculously nursed him back to life. He also liked to chase cars and we had no success in breaking him of that dangerous habit. I feared that one day it would really do him in. Even though he never learned his lesson, and continued to chase cars and pick fights, he lived on, stout-hearted indeed. It was years later, when I was in college, that I received the devastating news that Fuzzy had succumbed to cancer. My girlhood companion was gone, leaving me sad for a long, long time.

WASHINGTON, D.C.

It wasn't until after I had returned from my tour of duty with the CIA in Vienna, was married and working in Washington, that dogs re-entered my life. Several dogs. Friends in St. Louis asked us to board their well-bred Doberman Pinschers while prospective buyers arranged for their purchase. Our small row house in Foggy Bottom, at the edge of a parking lot, was a crowded way station and suffered some minor damages from its four-legged guests, but we became enamored of the breed and soon after the boarders had gone, my husband and I set out to buy our own Doberman.

Hasso, our first, was a spirited animal. I took him on evening walks, which he liked to turn into runs, down 23rd Street, and over to an open area on C Street. We would pass the last self-standing house on the block, on the other side of the parking lot from our house, where the "Dutchess" lived. She was a handsome black woman with somewhat of a reputation and several children whom I used to invite over to pick the zinnias that grew in abundance in my front plot. Here Hasso was wont to lift his leg. I would try valiantly to curb him, but eighty pounds of Doberman made for a determined force and he would win out. Besides, that front yard was overgrown with weeds so his trespassing didn't seem too damaging. Until one time when the "Dutchess" came roaring from the back of her house, onto the porch, shouting,

"Don't let that dog pee on my flawrs!" I looked down at the inde-
structible milkweed, at a loss to see the harm, but quickly agreed—
her yard, so, OK, they could be her flowers—and thereafter, I
walked on the other side of the street.

When my husband graduated from George Washington
University, he wanted to get back into the intelligence game. The
CIA was under a hiring freeze at the time so Bob took a job with a
civilian intelligence agency at the Defense Department that soon
sent us to Munich, Germany, where we were housed in Army
quarters in an area called Perlacher Forest. I was told I had to
resign my permanent position with the CIA if I accompanied my
husband, so of course I resigned, although I never understood the
logic or the fairness of that requirement. Fortunately, I was
picked up on contract status at the CIA station there, so we both
were back in business.

MUNICH, GERMANY

Hasso came with us and through him we met German
Doberman breeders. One such couple in particular became fast
friends. We learned much about the breed from the Schroeters
and had the opportunity to watch Herr Schroeter trim and tie up
the ears of his new born puppies. Dobermans are born with
hound's ears that must be shaped into the stand-up ears by which
the breed is recognized and their long tails are docked. They are
handsome dogs whose original stock was crossed with cattle dogs
that were used to drive northward the cattle bought in
Switzerland and southern Germany. Their intelligence, alertness
and powerful bodies make them especially suited to perform vari-

ous types of useful work, often without any regular training. We liked them because they also made affectionate house dogs as well as excellent watch dogs and we preferred males with red and tan coloring instead of the black and tan markings.

Unfortunately, we were not able to take Hasso back to the States with us when our tour of duty was over. Our Doberman friends found him a good home, and we returned, ready for a new, and different, assignment. That eventually turned out to be another overseas job. But, in the meantime, we spent anxious days waiting for the clearances and arrangements that had to be made.

CHARLOTTESVILLE, VIRGINIA

We bided the time in Charlottesville, Virginia, where my parents had moved from Illinois. Dad had retired from his job at Shell Oil Company in Wood River, and mother thought she had retired as well, but was recruited to be a substitute teacher at an elementary school just a couple of blocks away from their new house. Then, when a first grade teacher resigned, mother was asked to take over the job full time. She did, and taught for ten more years! Her remarkable record was enviable; no child ever left her class without having learned to read.

Bob and I stayed at first with mother and dad, then moved into a big, comfortable farmhouse, Cherry Hill, a short way west of Charlottesville. It was across the road from where Peter Jefferson's Shadwell plantation, a once thriving agricultural estate, was located and where Thomas Jefferson was born and lived much of his early life. We had acquired another Dobie, named Baron, whom we affectionately called Roon; he would be with us a long time. He loved the farm where he could race around in the fields and pastures and where he had a number of encounters with skunks and, subsequently, a number of baths in tomato juice that really worked in getting rid of the smell.

I enrolled him in obedience school, an education that taught me more than I seemed to be able to teach him, but he did, finally, learn to heel, sit and stay. When he was thus ready for walking in the city, I took him to the University of Virginia campus and together we would stroll along the serpentine walls and around the quadrangle, past Poe's cell-like room where a raven perched ominously in the window.

One evening in May,1962, I went with Mother and Dad to a program at Old Cabell Hall at the University. William Faulkner was again at the university as the Balch lecturer in American Literature and was to make another public appearance. He had already made two such appearances and his final one was scheduled for May 17*. That evening was the highlight of my Charlottesville days.

The hall was crowded and we finally found seats in the first row of the balcony, an excellent vantage point from which to hear and see. Mr. Faulkner looked so distinguished in his white suit and read, in his soft, southern voice, from *The Reivers,* his newly published and, sadly, last book. There was a large and enthusiastic audience in attendance. He took questions afterwards and I remember standing up at my balcony seat, holding on to the railing to steady myself and asking one, but I cannot remember what it was! However, I do recall how nervous I felt at my audacity and how elated I was to hear him reply, so courteously—to me! As we

---

*Joseph Blotner, *Faulkner, A Biography, Vol 2* (New York: Random House, Inc., 1974), p.1822.

three left the hall after the program and were walking through the parking lot to our car, I spotted Mr. Faulkner standing by the side of a car, relaxing with a couple of other men. As I passed by, I impulsively gave a little wave and he responded by lifting a flask in a sort of salute—a gracious gesture from a gracious gentleman. We exchanged smiles.

At last the day came when my husband and I were to depart. We were headed back to Munich, this time to live on the economy as an American business couple. Bob would be a representative of a restaurant equipment company in New York City and I was to be the good *Hausfrau*. In late summer, we sailed in style aboard the S.S. *America* from New York to Genoa and Baron lived the life of Riley on board, feasting on steak and other treats. I worried if he would ever want dog food again. We visited him daily in his lair, and ran with him around the top deck—good exercise for us, as well.

Upon arriving in Genoa, we found ourselves the subject of intense interest from the Italian customs officials who were preparing to inspect each of our two trunks, three rifles and eighteen pieces of hand luggage—small wonder! It was obvious our clearance would take forever and the line behind us was as restive as we were. But at this point, Baron came to the rescue. As the officials debated where to start, Baron, without any prompting, pulled me along on his leash up to the first piece of our luggage for which the officious inspector had just demanded the key and emitted a snarl such as I had never heard before. It was accompanied by a show of teeth I had never seen before either. The wide-eyed officials stared ever so briefly at the growling dog and, suddenly, in great haste, began stamping every piece of our baggage without opening one! They waved us through with looks of relief and called after us good wishes for a safe trip, or maybe it was good riddance, or worse. In any event, it was the quickest customs clearance ever.

Our next obstacle was fitting all this into the miniature taxis waiting at the dock. We needed two and still had to put some baggage on top. Bob rode in the lead cab with his guns and I squeezed into the second one with the dog. We zipped off to the railroad station, taking corners on two wheels. I could hear the cargo shifting above and feared we would tip over, but all I could do was hold on tight. We made it to the station intact and began the unloading process, then paraded through the station looking like celebrities—we two with guns and dog followed by porters pushing three luggage carts.

At long last, we were ensconced in our compartment on our way to Munich. We fed Baron and went off to the dining car. Upon our return, we found our dog stretched out on the lower bunk and nothing would entice him to relinquish his perch. Defeated, the two of us spent a less than restful night together in the top berth.

RETURN TO MUNICH

Getting settled in Munich was a long process. After a prolonged hotel stay, during which we shared a room with Baron, we found a perfect place to live, the second floor apartment in a two-family house on the *Karl Valentin Strasse* in Grünwald, a charming suburb south of Munich. The town was reachable by a scenic streetcar ride from the city on tram line No. 25. It went past the Bavaria Film Studio and, at the last stop, one got off near a little cinema that showed vintage films. I saw lots of Charlie Chaplin movies there— *The Great Dictator,* and *City Lights*, my favorite, among others. It seemed a happy coincidence that the person after whom our street was named was considered the Chaplin of Germany!

Furnishing our new place was a chore. I was still dead tired from the trip but drug myself along on our exhausting shopping forays. One particular day found us searching for a lamp in a rambling electric appliance store. While Bob roamed around, I leaned against a pillar on the main floor to wait for him and found myself gradually slipping down to the floor where I just wanted to stay forever. I had never felt so overwhelmingly tired. Nothing seemed to matter as I drifted off to sleep. I was finally discovered curled up at the base of the column and my husband had to half carry, half drag me home. Shortly afterwards, I miscarried. I was devastated for we had wanted to start a family for so long and had had no success. However, I consoled myself with the knowledge that at least now I knew that I could get pregnant.

Another comforting thing about this was finding Herr Doktor Schrader, a gynecologist whose care and concern got me through this experience and gave me hope for a future pregnancy. He was recommended by a newly-made German friend, a sympathetic woman who became a good friend. And so, within the first weeks of our arrival in Munich, I found myself in Dr. Schrader's basement operating room in his *Klinik*, a small, spotless facility overlooking the Isar River. In faultless English, he took time to explain to uninitiated me the procedure he would perform—dilation and curettage—and advised me to stay a day or two at the *Klinik*, to "regain my strength." That stay certainly proved therapeutic. The nurses were most solicitous and comforting and twice daily brought me a glass of beer that the doctor had prescribed. New friends brought flowers that the nurses removed at bedtime so they wouldn't "poison the night air!" Thus recovered, I left re-charged and ready to tackle the onerous task of unpacking and settling-in.

Salesman Bob began traveling around Germany a lot on business while I served as his stay-at-home support structure. I was lonely at times, with no friends to talk to, but busied myself with household chores and letter writing. I became the consummate *Hausfrau* with Baron as my constant companion. Together we went on runs and walks—on errands to the butcher's, the baker's, and the greengrocer's almost every day. Baron knew our shopping itinerary as well as I and I often thought I could have sent him thither with a note and he, working class dog that he was, would return with my orders!

Baron never tired of our routine and I enjoyed the exercise with him, but I tired of the purchases I brought home. I grew weary of sausages and schnitzels and root vegetables, and decided I had to vary our diet. But where to find anything different? We ate out sometimes at a nearby Chinese restaurant and it occurred to me: that's it! I'll learn to cook Chinese! But I would need a Chinese cookbook. I drove to the American Army hospital where there was a small newsstand and bookstore. There I found just what I was looking for: *The Art of Chinese Cooking* by the Benedictine Sisters of Peking. From then on, both Bob and I specialized in Chinese cuisine and Baron and I drove downtown to buy the bean sprouts, bamboo shoots, ginger, and all the other ingredients readily available in Munich's Chinatown. My diet depression disappeared.

When Baron wasn't out with me, shopping or exercising, he would explore our section of the back yard. We shared the yard and the garage with our downstairs neighbors, Herr and Frau Huber. He was in the ladies' lingerie business and she was mother to two little girls, with a third baby on the way. It was hard to keep Baron in our part of the yard and it was a challenge to manage the garaging arrangements. The garage was built one car-width wide and two car-lengths deep so one car had to be parked ahead of the other. Somehow, we all succeeded in getting in and out without too much confusion and our neighbors were quite cooperative.

One day while Bob was cutting grass, Baron was engaged in an exhausting game of bring back the ball. One throw of mine went a bit too far and rolled behind the bushes next to a fence. Baron wiggled down under the shrubbery and quickly emerged with something in his mouth, but it wasn't his red ball. It was, however, round, and he proudly deposited it at my feet. It moved slightly. Baron was transfixed. Then he toyed with it, batting it away and pushing it back with his snout. This game was such fun! Then, he tried to pick it up again. He managed to get it partially into his mouth before letting out a searing howl of pain.

"What is that?" I called to Bob, who came running to investigate.

"I think, I think, oh no, it's an *Igel!*"

Baron had been playing with a porcupine that had obviously put up its defenses. The dog's muzzle looked like a pincushion and he lay on the ground with quills in his front paws as well. We tried to remove them but only succeeded in causing the poor animal more pain. We would have to take him to the veterinarian. And carry him to the car because, clearly, Baron couldn't walk. The neighbors obligingly moved their car so we could back out ours and Bob and I struggled to lift our eighty-five pound Doberman into the back seat. I sat there with him and put his head in my lap and tried to comfort him. Even though Baron whimpered all the way, I thought of him as very brave. Finally we delivered him to the vet who removed the hurtful quills and required him to stay overnight. That was all right, except that Bob would be leaving town on the morrow and I would have to fetch Baron by myself.

The next day, the vet and I wrestled Baron onto the car's back seat. His front paws were all bandaged up and his muzzle looked pock-marked from the plucking of the quills. The vet's parting instructions were that Baron should have soft food and must stay off his feet until his return visit in a week—exactly the length of time that Bob would be away! I drove off while Baron lay still, trying to lick his paws. I was relieved that he didn't try to chew off the bandages.

Keeping the dog off his feet and getting him up to our apartment posed the first big challenge. I had brought along a thick old throw rug on which to transport him from car to front door and managed, by pulling, pushing, and lifting to extricate Baron from the back seat and position him on the rug. He rode in grand style to the door as I tugged the rug along the walkway and into the stairwell. Then, I pondered the next move.

Baron seemed as perplexed as I as I sat on the bottom step to pet him and to think of a way to get him upstairs. The only solution that came to mind was to hold him on my lap and move up the stairs sitting on my bottom! Somehow it worked and once inside, I put him back on the rug and pulled him to his bed where I had placed his water and food dishes. This became our mode of locomotion each day—two or three times up and down the stairs by the seat of my pants with Baron sprawled on my lap, head hanging over my shoulder. Once outside, though, he had to stand on all fours and raise his leg, a painful procedure. Bob returned a day early, thankfully, and together we took the dog back for his check up. The veterinarian pronounced him healed and ready to walk and chew again; an enormous relief—for both the dog and me!

Winter roared in with the new year and brought one of the snowiest seasons in decades. The field in the block in front of our house was a canvas of white waiting to be decorated and Baron did just that. Back and forth he would plow, pushing through the snow as high as his chest, leaving a beautiful pattern of criss-crosses and circles and yellow spots in his wake. He frolicked while I froze.

One frigid day, as I glanced from our bedroom window, I saw Frau Huber trudging across the field, pulling a child's sled behind her. On it was balanced a small suitcase; she was on her way to the local *Klinik* to deliver her third baby. I wanted to rejoice for her but could only feel sorry for myself. How unfair it seemed, that she could have children and I couldn't!

Soon after that, as if my jealous prayers had been answered, I discovered I was pregnant again. I wanted to take to my bed in some misguided attempt to insure that nothing would happen to this pregnancy. That was impossible, of course, but I became super careful and even dreaded walking Baron for fear he would jerk me down on the ground, something that had never happened. In fact, he was most obedient on our excursions, heeling and stopping on orders and walking slowly on the slippery surfaces as if sensing my reluctance in navigating on the snow and ice.

One cold day, when Bob was away, I holed up in our cozy apartment, satisfied that all was well. But it wasn't. Late that afternoon, I experienced that familiar overpowering feeling of tiredness followed by an urgent need to use the toilet. Smoothly, silently, the fetus slipped out. I stared into the bowl, disbelievingly, and saw the tiny shape, floating now in unwelcoming water. I stood there, stunned and weak, and wept as it was washed away along with my tears. I crept into bed and lay there, exhausted, alone and ineffably sad. I began to sob. Suddenly, I felt the weight of something on my sodden pillow and turned to receive a gentle nudge from Baron's muzzle. His luminous eyes looked sad as he nuzzled me and made soothing sounds, as if he understood my sorrow, as if to say now it's his turn to take care of me. I hugged him and stroked his smooth head and the soft skin at the back of his neck. I spoke his name, over and over.

I lay there for a long time, not wanting to move, but it was almost dark and I knew I had to get up and make my way to a telephone to call Dr. Schrader. We had been told when we moved in that we would not be able to get phone service for at least nine months and we were still waiting. I was struck at the thought of this ironic interval. Finally, I managed to get up and dressed for the weather. Equipped with flashlight, German coins and accompanied by my faithful escort, I staggered out into the cold.

Breath seemed to freeze on my face as Baron and I struggled to walk side by side through the narrow tunnel of snow piled up as high as my head on either side of the path. Icy branches made a sparkling arbor above us. At last we came to the phone booth standing in a barely cleared space surrounded by snow banks. There was no street light, but after tugging at the door, it opened and triggered the glow of what had to be no more than a twenty-watt bulb. Since the space inside the booth was so small, I told Baron to wait outside. He clearly did not want to do so and made such a commotion I had to let him in.

But that made things extremely difficult. I was standing on the platform that activated the phone. It was like an old fashioned scale at a country fair, the kind one stepped on to start the process that produced a little card with one's weight on it. But this wasn't a fun outing and there was no room on this platform for all of our six feet for Baron kept trying to gain a purchase on it. Even when I moved to the side, he could manage just two paws on the platform before he would slide off or would force me off. It occurred to me that this routine would have been really funny under other circumstances; now, it was just exasperating. At last I managed to position him with his rear end on the platform and paws in the narrow space between the platform and the door.

"Stay," I commanded, summoning my most authoritative voice. And he did.

By now the booth was completely steamed up and I could barely see. It smelled of wet wool and doggy breath and I felt slightly nauseous and claustrophobic in our cramped quarters. I tried to balance the flashlight on top of the phone box so I could see better, but it wouldn't stay so I was forced to squint in the dim light from above. My fingers were stiff within my gloves that had to come off so I could try to extricate the coins from my pocket. I finally retrieved a mark and just as I was aiming to drop it into the slot, Baron inched closer, causing me to lose my balance and stumble off the platform. The coin fell to the dark ground. After a flashlight search that engendered much switching of positions, I found the money and resettled the dog. I felt so weary and frustrated and cold and was desperate to talk with my gynecologist.

It took two more unsuccessful tries, but, finally, I managed to get the money in the slot and the call went through. Dr. Schrader answered right away, to my immense relief. He calmed me and tried to reassure me and told me to come to his *Klinik* within the next couple of days. I felt much better after talking with him. Baron and I stumbled out of the booth that now seemed so warm compared to the blast of cold air that met us outside. Shivering, we carefully picked our icy way home and I crawled back in bed. Baron stayed with me all night, curled up on the rug by the side of the bed and every so often he got up to nuzzle me again, to make sure I was all right. He seemed to sense my despondent state and offered me what comfort he could. It was enough; his devoted presence truly consoled me, our connectedness was cemented in sympathy.

The next day, Bob was back. He shared my disappointment over the miscarriage but was much more sanguine than I at our future prospects for children. He delivered me to the *Klinik* and was told he could return later to see me after the procedure. I relaxed on the gurney as I was wheeled away by two nurses to Dr. Schrader's operating room, feeling quite floaty from the effects of the pre-*narkose* drug they had administered. The two of them were chatting away as they pushed me into the elevator and hit a button.

I had the impression that I was riding up, instead of down to Dr. Schrader's basement room and, with heightened awareness, I heard one say, *"Sie is hier für eine Blinddarmoperation, nicht wahr?"*

"Ja, ja," replied the other, with complete conviction.

At this, I bolted upright, now fully alarmed, and shouted, *"Nein, nein! Ich muss nach unten gehen—runter, zu Herrn Doktor Schrader—für eine D und C!"* They were as surprised as I when I made it clear that I was not there for an appendectomy! Thank heavens I had been aware enough to understand them. Meanwhile, Dr. Schrader had been frantically searching for his lost patient and was extremely relieved to see me. The reaction was mutual!

Summer arrived and so did our telephone! We discovered all over again how comforting it felt to be connected with the outer world. Bob was busy and would spend evenings typing up reports, reports I was not allowed to see. This didn't bother me all that much since I was preoccupied with my pregnancy problem. I would settle myself on the sofa to read or watch re-runs of the old

Topper movies, enjoying the timeless sophistication of Myrna Loy and William Powell while being warmed by Baron, curled up at my feet—actually, spread out on top of them in a position he found comfortable and I found cozy.

Our social life revolved around our German friends. We drove an Audi and became sports car enthusiasts. Bob founded the Bavarian Sports Car Club and organized gymkannas and races on an abandoned airport runway. He also planned treasure hunts via automobile. These were lots of fun until the driver chastised the navigator for missing a checkpoint and, at the post-hunt festivities, many a couple was not speaking to each other. Once in a rare while, we went, literally under cover of darkness, to visit American friends, our former colleagues. These few outings really raised our morale, despite their being more or less *verboten*.

One November evening there was a knock at our door. I put down my book to see who was there and was surprised to find our downstairs neighbors, teary eyed and clearly shaken. I asked them in, fearing that something terrible had happened to them or to their little girls. But they had come to offer their sympathies to us. They brought the horrible news that President Kennedy had been assassinated.

We had not been watching TV nor listening to the radio and were stunned to hear of this national tragedy. The Hubers were as devastated as we for the Germans held Kennedy in such high regard.

"The President, our hero, gone," they lamented.

We commiserated together with stiff drinks and offered a final toast to the man who had once declared in solidarity, even if incorrectly, *"Ich bin ein Berliner."* The next day, Bob and I went to the American Consulate in Munich to sign the condolence book and stood in the cold, cold weather for hours along with hundreds of mourning Münchners who had formed a line that stretched for blocks.

Later that winter, there was, sadly, yet another visit to Dr. Schrader's operating room. Once more, I had been so hopeful. I had been having dreams of actually delivering a baby. This recurrent dream was so real that I imagined pain and would awake, sweating, half expecting it to be true. So when I became pregnant again, I was convinced that the old adage, the third time is a charm, would work for me. But after the third miscarriage in almost two years, the doctor prescribed "anti-baby" pills, as he termed the contraceptives, and ordered me not to get pregnant again for at least several months. I was, as he pointed out, quite run down and should build myself up before trying again. I followed his advice—for a while.

RETURN TO CHARLOTTESVILLE

When Bob's two-year stint was up, he and I, accompanied by Baron, sailed back to the United States, heading for Charlottesville, Virginia. We planned to visit with my parents there for a couple of weeks, then go on to Boston, to see Bob's parents. We arrived in Charlottesville in the midst of a glorious autumn—the weather was crisp and cool, the foliage was turning, and the hunting season for pheasants was on. Bob headed out to the cornfields, to shoot with a friend; he returned, carried by the friend, with a broken heel. He had jumped across a little stream and landed on what he thought was a mossy patch but turned out to be a moss-covered rock The crack of his bone sounded like a shot and for a moment both he and his friend had thought his gun had gone off and he had shot himself in the foot. Very carefully, and very painfully for Bob, we cut off his boot and rushed him to the hospital.

The cast encompassed his leg from the toes to the thigh and our two-week visit turned into a months-long stay. This was, on the whole, a wonderful time—I was back in the nest, free from all the anxieties of our recent life and oh, so ready to be taken care of by my mother, who also cared for Bob. And, once it became known that I was pregnant again—quite an accomplishment considering the cast and all—dad took over the care of Baron. The two of them took long walks and then would perch, side by side, on the top of the steep bank, covered in honeysuckle vines, in front of the house to watch the cars go by. Watching them watch the cars was like following a tennis match in slow motion—their heads would turn to the left as they spotted an approaching car, then swivel smoothly to the right as it passed. And repeat. They even talked to one another.

Dad would say, "Here comes a Chevy, see it, Roon?" And I could swear that Baron nodded in agreement and gave a little "woof." They were such pals.

The weeks wore by with all of us holding our collective breath. But I was growing and glowing, confident that all would be well this time what with Dad's taking over dog duty and Mother's dispensing the only "medicine" the doctor prescribed—a daily glass of orange juice—freshly squeezed.

Christmas came and would have been even merrier if Bob had had a new job lined up. He kept busy selling British cars at S-K Motors and I worked part-time in the library of Rock Hill Academy, a newly formed school, arranging books donated by parents and friends of the students. Dad drove me back and forth and insisted on putting the volumes on the top shelves so I wouldn't stretch or, worse, fall off the ladder. Despite our happiness over the expected baby, uncertainty loomed ahead. Because of another hiring freeze, prospects were bleak for Bob's ever joining the Company, so he began a job search in new directions. Regrettably, our spying days were over, and the time had come to move on.

And move on we did—to Boston where Bob began a career with the Bank of Boston. He left Charlottesville in late winter, as soon as he was able to drive. I was to follow after Easter. We would stay with his parents until we could build our own home. Happy days were here again! However, my euphoria was short lived for I soon learned I couldn't bring Baron along when I went to Boston—Bob's parents already had a dog, a yappy, hairy little Sheltie, and didn't want a big Doberman around. We couldn't afford to kennel Roon, which would not have been good for him anyway, so I faced the realization that my beloved Baron and I would have to part.

The very thought made me extremely sad; he was my bosom companion, a member of the family along with Mother and Dad. The rupture haunted me and worried my parents as well. Then mother discovered that a friend of hers knew someone who might, just might, want a working class dog, such as a Doberman, to guard her show horses. And so it was that we found ourselves, one spring afternoon, sitting on the patio at Knole Farm, sipping soft drinks and discussing with Jill Faulkner Summers the prospect of leaving Baron in the care of her horse trainer. Arrangements were quickly made, and we left with plans to return with Baron shortly after Easter.

Even though I knew Baron would have a good home, and he certainly did, I could barely say goodbye when the time came. I cried for three days afterwards. I longed to stroke his brown coat once more, to have him sit on my feet again and warm me all over. But I had left Charlottesville and now we were miles apart.

Soon my sadness at leaving Baron was replaced by the joy of the birth of our daughter, Andrea. We were living in our new house in Wenham, MA, after a stay with Bob's parents. We were a happy little family; nonetheless, I eagerly awaited the letters the trainer so kindly wrote me about Baron's new life. Baron slept in the tack house with the trainer and traveled with him to the horse shows where he performed his guard duties admirably. Baron also learned to bring the horses up from the pasture and into the barn! What an amazing dog he proved to be, but I was not surprised—he was true to his heritage.

We went back often to Charlottesville to visit my parents and on one trip, when my daughter was two and a half, Mother arranged for us to visit Knole Farm and see Baron. I was so excited and delighted that I could introduce little Andrea to my favorite four-legged friend. I was also wondering if he would remember me and hoped hard that he would. It was late afternoon of a lovely summer's day when we walked out to the pasture to watch Baron bring up the horses. From far away, I saw him loping along and then, all of a sudden, stop and, nose in the air, sniff something on the wind. For a moment he stood perfectly still and then took off pell-mell towards us! He was running in my direction at full gallop and was soon upon me, up on his hind legs with his front paws on my shoulders, licking my face in joyous greeting. Baron remembered me! I was overjoyed and, released from his doggie embrace, knelt down to hug him around his neck and pet him, all the while whispering, "Roon, Roon," over and over again.

Mother had grabbed Andrea's hand and backed away when she saw Baron racing towards us, but now came up to pet him, too. Baron responded warmly, wiggling his hindquarters and his stub of a tail and laying his ears flat against his head. Mother patted him in her familiar way—he remembered her too. And now, Baron saw Andrea, this strange, small person whom he didn't know. He slowly approached her while she stood quite still, wanting to welcome him as we did, but not really sure what to expect from an encounter with this big dog. I was at her side and helped her gingerly pat his head. Baron sensed her smallness and nuzzled her neck ever so gently, then sat down beside her, he as tall as she, and rested his head on her shoulder. Andrea put her arms around his neck, and they became fast friends as well. How intuitive Baron's actions, how perfectly appropriate his greetings for each of us.

The moment is etched in my memory, one of my most treasured remembrances. I have thought of this reunion so many times and especially when, years later, I received what was to be the last of the letters from his keeper. Baron, he wrote, had developed cancer of the mouth and had to be put down. I grieved a very long time and miss him still.

LUXEMBOURG CITY, LUXEMBOURG

Bob's assignments with the Bank of Boston took us abroad again. He had proposed the establishment of a branch of the bank in Luxembourg where favorable tax laws, numbered accounts, and low costs were attracting foreign banks. His plan was accepted and the Bank of Boston became the first foreign bank to operate there. Moreover, its arrival was to serve as the first step in the development of Luxembourg as a banking and administrative center in Europe. Luxembourg City became, in fact, a banking boom town.

In August 1970, our family, now four with the happy addition of our son Robbie, set sail for Europe, bag, baggage, and automobile. We drove from Le Harve to Luxembourg, described by the guide books as embodying the best of romantic Europe within its borders. The delightful little Duchy boasts a diverse topography: there are high hills and broad plains, lovely little medieval villages, picture book castles, and wineries. Luxembourg City itself is perched atop precipitous cliffs that drop into the narrow valleys of the Petrusse and Alzette rivers.

We found the whole country most welcoming to Americans. We spent a few days ensconced in comfortable rooms at the Grand Cravat, a prominent hotel in downtown Luxembourg City. However, living at the "Big Tie," as we nicknamed it, proved difficult for the children and as well as for their mother. For one thing, while room service for breakfast was great, there would arrive hot milk for the children's cold cereal. This was just a minor inconvenience, but the main problem was that there was no place for them to play and I had run out of ideas and patience. So, it was decided that we three should spend a few weeks out of town until a new home could be found.

Bob had fortunately made the acquaintance of a local family who graciously offered us the use of their home in Clervaux as well as an apartment in Blankenberge on the Belgian coast. It was agreed: Bob would stay on at the hotel to begin the daunting task of organizing the bank and would visit us on weekends; the children and I would go first to the coast.

We boarded a train for the day trip that would take us there via Brussels. I was bogged down with baggage for the two-week stay. I had everything I could possibly need—or carry—except for the most important item of all—Pampers! The footlocker containing that precious cargo had not yet been forwarded from the ship. I would have to make do with the emergency cloth diapers I had luckily packed before leaving the states and felt certain that I could find a Pampers-like product in Blankenberge.

We were joined in our compartment by a Belgian businessman who was returning to Brussels. We began to chat while Andrea, just a couple of weeks shy of her fifth birthday, and Robbie, two and a half, busied themselves with books and crayons and the few little toys I had tucked into my tote. Time flew by as quickly as the train raced along. As we approached Brussels, I realized the interval for changing trains was terribly tight and that I could easily miss the connection. My alarming discovery alerted my fellow traveler. He checked the track numbers and confirmed that it would be extremely difficult for me to catch the connecting train.

"But I can help you," he volunteered. "I get off here, so I have the time."

I quickly accepted his kind offer, and even though I was still doubtful I was willing to make a run for it, given his assistance. I really didn't want to be stranded in the station. We loaded up and were ready to detrain when I realized we had entered the station several tracks away from the one we needed to get to and that if we walked, or even ran, along on the platforms, we would never make it. My companion saw the problem as well.

He suddenly jumped down from the doorway and yelled, "Follow me." Scooping up Robbie, whom he carried under his arm like a football, and grabbing one of my suitcases along with his briefcase, he began leaping across the tracks with the agility of an athlete. I slung my purse over my chest, bandolier style, and hooked my huge tote bag over my shoulder so I could grab Andrea's hand. I picked up the other suitcase with my free hand and struggled to follow. I had to lift Andrea up over the rails as we tried to run and hop along. I prayed I wouldn't stumble nor pull her arm out of its socket.

There were no trains on the tracks we were traversing, but when I dared a quick look around I saw to my horror that one was entering the station. It was still a little way off, but I had to beat it. My poor little girl was frightened and holding on for dear life. Ahead of us, there were two more tracks, quite far apart, to cross. The Belgian, with Robbie still safely under his arm, was approaching the track our train was waiting on. It's engine was huffing and puffing, sounding like it was getting ready to move. I summoned up a last burst of strength and somehow, with superhuman effort, straggled across the track on which the approaching train was chugging in, closer than I had thought, and forced myself on, pulling Andrea along across the next track.

Just as I closed in on the last track, where the train to the coast was chuffing, I dropped the suitcase. I hollered for Andrea to run to the platform where my helper was waving frantically for me to hurry. She darted on and he pulled her up out of the track bed as I stumbled over and heaved my suitcase onto the platform. The conductor, a few cars away, was calling out what had to be "All aboard" and I heard "Blankenberge" so we were, at last, at the right place. The Belgian lifted Andrea up on the steps, then Robbie. They stood there, anxious for me to join them. I clambered aboard and our helper shoved up the suitcases. I had time only to shout, "Thank you, thank you so much" before we were underway. He waved back and soon disappeared from sight. I herded bags and kids into an empty compartment and collapsed. We were exhausted from our harrowing crossing and rested the rest of the way, so grateful for the kindness of that stranger.

The attractive apartment in Blankenberge was on the third

floor of a building right on the water. Perfect! Madame Hansen, whose guests we were, had an apartment nearby and joined us almost every day at the beach. The children loved the sand and the ocean, as cold here as it was on the coast of Massachusetts. This was no obstacle to their enjoyment of the seaside, however, nor to mine, although I preferred to sit under an umbrella and simply relax.

For I was mostly tired, what with grocery shopping every day with children in tow, then fixing meals they would eat. But the worst chore was doing the laundry. I never did locate anything resembling a laundromat, and had to resort to using the bathtub. I washed out everything there by hand, including diapers, and draped the wet things on every possible surface and chair back. This made the whole place damp—and dreary. One day, though, I ran out of the cloth diapers; the ones I'd washed were drying too slowly, so that morning's food foray was going to focus on finding disposable diapers. I was doubly desperate to do so because Madame Hansen, whose apartment had a telephone, had relayed a message from Bob saying he couldn't get away to see us that weekend and, anyway, the anxiously awaited footlocker had not yet arrived. Bob would, however, be coming the second weekend to drive us to Clervaux, our next temporary lodging.

"Oh, dear God, not another week of back-breaking bending over the bath tub!" was all I could think upon hearing this disappointing information. As a treat, more for myself than for the kids, I proposed we eat out for lunch. I found a suitable restaurant on the way to the town center and relished the glass of incomparable Belgian beer I ordered along with the omelets and salads and milk for the children. Thus fortified, I set out for the shops. I was hurrying along, holding Robbie's hand; Andrea was dawdling, yet I assumed she was right behind me. But she wasn't.

I heard her cry out, and turned around to see her some ways back—stuck in a sidewalk grate! One foot was caught between the grates and try as I did, I couldn't dislodge it. My poor daughter! I felt awful. I should have been holding her hand as well but so single-minded was I about my mission that I assumed, wrongly, that she would catch up and walk beside me. Several passersby stopped to help and finally one man freed her foot, after twisting and turning it until I feared her ankle would be broken. Andrea hobbled along gamely as I resumed the march downtown.

A small variety store seemed promising. I roamed the aisles until I came across a counter bearing baby goods. And there was a package that looked like it held disposable diapers. I bought it without hesitation. After some grocery shopping, we made our weary way back to the apartment, up the three flights of stairs, and that evening I inaugurated the new diaper. It was unusually narrow and straight and there was no elastic around the legs but I was desperate—I certainly didn't want to defeat the diaper's purpose by using a really damp cloth one. Alas, by morning it was obvious I had made the wrong decision. Of course, elastic around the legs is a necessary feature and so is a wide cut shaped to fit! Now, not only did I have a royal mess to clean up, I had the sheets and nightclothes to wash as well. By this time, my knuckles and knees were red, my fingers wrinkled, my back hurt, and my disposition was bad. Those disposable diapers I'd bought were indeed disposable but useless for the purpose for which they were—so badly—designed. However, rather than throw them away I figured I could use them as crib pads.

We went back to the beach the next day to escape the dank apartment. The weather was so delightful and the sea air so refreshing that my mood improved greatly. Mme. Hansen and I were drowsing in our chairs under an umbrella, lazily watching Robbie and Andrea play in the sand. When Robbie ventured down to the water's edge, I forced myself up to follow. I'm not sure Mme. Hansen knew I had left and perhaps she had dosed off for when I came back with Robbie, Andrea was nowhere in sight. In a panic, I raced back to the water, praying she hadn't waded in although I felt sure she hadn't—I certainly would have seen her there.

I shouted to Mme. Hansen to watch Robbie and ran to the boardwalk, hoping that was where Andrea would have walked along, but in which direction? I headed to the right, toward the farthest end of the beach, calling her name even though it was drowned out by all the seaside sounds. I stopped to ask several sunbathers if they had seen a little girl in a pink bathing suit. Even though I couldn't make myself understood in Dutch, Flemish, or even French, my urgent gestures and frantic appearance gave the people a good idea of what was wrong and they started to look around and call out my daughter's name.

My fear was that she had been whisked away by someone. The word kidnapped came to mind. Yet, as I calmed down a bit, I assured myself that she must have just wandered off. I ran on, and eventually saw, in the distance, a Red Cross tent.

"Please God, let her be there," I prayed.

I was panting as I entered the tent. The Red Cross worker could spot a distraught mother right away and she motioned me over to where she was sitting and where my dear, dear daughter was holding court! "Little Miss Magpie" was chattering away and eating cookies, perfectly composed and enjoying all the attention. She was very happy to see me and wondered why I looked so worried—she had just wanted to go exploring! After hugs and kisses, I tried to explain why what she had done was so worrisome and hoped she had learned a lesson about "running away."

That weekend Bob arrived—with the footlocker full of disposable diapers! I'm not sure whether I was happier to see him or what he brought! After a last day at the beach, we drove off to Luxembourg where I would spend another two weeks with the children—in Clervaux. This lovely medieval market town, sunk into a narrow valley along the river Clerve in the heart of the Ardennes in the north of the country, is the home of the ancient Benedictine Abbey that sits atop a hill overlooking the valley. The original structure was built in the 12th century and was the home of St. Bernard de Clervaux who died there in 1183 leaving his hymns to live on.

Our *pied-à-terre*, Mme. Hansen's house, was on the road up to the Abbey and I had always intended to visit there, but had never found the time. I was told the Abbey had been restored to its pre-war condition after being destroyed during the Battle of the Bulge. That ferocious battle, one of the largest and bloodiest of World War II, raged throughout the area in the bitter winter of December, 1944, the coldest winter in memory, and continued until mid-January, 1945, when the Allies finally fought back the bulge the Germans had caused in the thinly held Allied line.

In a small park on the side of a hill in the town there stands a Patton tank, the one, it's said, that defended Clervaux's chateau as the savage struggle spread into the town. General George S. Patton, who commanded the Third Army in the campaign, was known for his first hand knowledge of tanks and his advocacy of their use so the presence of the tank in that place seemed a fitting tribute to him. It also stands as a reminder of all the courageous U.S. troops who fought during the Bulge and of the 19,000 who died.

One of those brave soldiers was my cousin, Don Hinrichs. As a

nineteen year old, Don went to war as a rifleman and machine gun-
ner with the 81st Combat Engineers of the 106th Infantry Division
that was attacked by the Germans in mid-December, 1944. Don
was ordered out on patrol in the St. Vith area early one frigid day
and set out so hurriedly he wore only a light jacket and socks that
had holes. The patrol became lost, but after several harrowing days,
was found and returned safely to the line. He was one of the soldiers who, thankfully, came home.

The parkette was a welcome stop on our treks up and down the
hill into town for both kids looked forward to climbing on the tank
there, an activity that was indeed allowed—I inquired to make sure.
Years later, when we lived in Manchester, MA, I would regularly
drive with the children over to Hamilton to take them to their piano
lessons and do errands. My route would take us past the town
green where there stood another Patton tank! I was surprised and
didn't learn till later that General Patton had owned a summer
home in Hamilton and that his son, Major General George Patton,
had retired there in 1980. The town of Hamilton dedicated its com-
mons to "Old Blood and Guts" and installed the tank there. What
were the odds of living near such a symbol on two continents? I relished this coincidence; Robbie liked to climb on that tank, too.

On one of our excursions down into town to do a little shopping, Andrea, who called herself Nan, was happily skipping along
the road, singing nursery rhymes. Suddenly, I heard an interesting
improvisation: "Nan be nimble, Nan be quick, Nan jump over—the
dog shit!" Which she did, thank goodness, but, while I was
impressed at her creativity, I wondered where she had learned such
a descriptive word. Maybe from me? When I encountered the
messy crib that day?

Almost all the amenities were available in Clervaux—green grocer, bakery, apothecary, restaurants, beauty shop—everything except, like Blankenburge, no place to do laundry. I shuddered at the thought of more bathtub battles and in my desperation, phoned Mme. Hansen, back in Luxembourg City, from the post office in town. She made an excellent suggestion. She told me of a swimming pool in a recreation area not too far from her house where we were staying. The pool had showers and—a washing machine! If I took the children for a swim, we would be eligible to use the shower room and the washer.

This seemed the perfect solution. The only catch was getting there. The road to the area boasted a couple of tortuous hairpin turns; it would have been much too dangerous—impossible—to walk there with children and laundry in tow. But, there was another way, a short cut straight down a steep, woodsy hill on the other side of the road from our house.

I set out one day with the children and a basket full of dirty clothes plus a bag with swimsuits and towels, and soap, snacks and purse. Andrea and Robbie were excited at the prospect of playing in the pool; I was worrying how I'd watch them and do the washing at the same time. The descent was tricky. The ground was uneven; there were roots and underbrush that tripped us and, in other places, loose dirt that made us slip. And the hill was indeed steep and long. Finally, we reached the bottom and made for the changing room. I put in a load of wash before we all got into the pool. I made the kids come out when I had to do another load. At last, the clothes were clean and the children and I changed for the climb ahead.

How could I not have realized that the wet wash would weigh a ton? I had planned to hang it all on the clothesline back at the house since there was no dryer at the pool site, but I hadn't thought through the interim step—the many, many steps it would take to struggle up the hill, like a beast of burden, with such a heavy load. I had to sit down to rest about half way up the hill, which now seemed more like a mountain to me. Everyone was hot and sweaty and my little charges were dirty from slipping and falling down, but they bravely soldiered on. I stumbled several times, too, but managed to keep the basket upright and the clean clothes clean. I groaned at the thought of baths all around again, once home. A final burst of energy got me there and I began immediately to hang up the washing on the clothesline outside. There weren't enough clothespins, so I just looped things over the line. It really didn't matter.

Finally back in the house and gulping down a glass of water, I decided that using the washing machine at the pool was a bad idea. I just couldn't go climbing again with a load of wet wash. But the bathtub alternative was equally unappealing. While mentally debating these choices, I glanced out the window to see if anything had fallen off the line. To my consternation the blue sky had clouded up and it was pouring rain! I simply didn't have the strength to even care and just let the washing get wetter.

I did undertake one more sally down the hill. The kids enjoyed the pool so much and I took along a much more selective, and lighter, load for the washer so the climb back wasn't so onerous the second time. We went back to play in the pool a couple more times, sans washing, which meant there was a big bag of laundry waiting for the trip back to Luxembourg City.

On weekends, we would station ourselves on the sofa next to the wide living room windows so we could watch for Bob on his drive up to the house, twirling around the hairpin turns in the "yellow bird," our canary yellow Camaro. On our last Sunday there, Mme. Hansen and her family arrived; they planned to stay in the house after we left. She would not let us leave on empty stomachs and proceeded to prepare a goodbye dinner for us. We gladly accepted her invitation. Everything was delicious, especially the light and airy dessert.

Bob complimented the cook, "Madam Hansen, this dessert is divine."

"Thank you, Mr. Perry. I'm so glad you like it," she replied, with a sly smile.

"What is it called?" Bob had to know.

Mme. Hansen paused for effect, then announced, "Nuns' farts!" She was delighted to observe our surprised reaction to the name of her heavenly concoction and we all laughed with her, especially the children who thought it was hilarious—actually, Bob and I did too.

Once back in the capital city, we had a short stay in a temporary house waiting for our new home to be ready. At last, we settled into an imposing town house across the street from the beautiful Stadtpark where the grand building that had been occupied by General Patton stood. It had served as his headquarters during the furious fighting that had raged all across the Ardennes.

Since Andrea had just turned five I enrolled her in a kindergarten. The school was located way across the *Pont Adolphe* that spanned the Petrusse valley, far from our townhouse in the Boulevard Prince Henri. I drove her there in the morning and picked her up in the afternoon. One day, I was a little late getting there, and didn't see her at our regular pick-up spot at the top of the hill although I had impressed upon her that she must always wait for me there. I drove down to the school building, thinking surely she must have waited there instead, but the nuns said she had left the classroom at the same time she always did.

They were puzzled, but I felt a pang of déjà vu, remembering the occurrence at the beach. That incident would prove to be but a minor scare compared to this disappearance. My stomach flip-flopped. Had she gone off by herself again? And then came the awful thought, had someone else picked her up? The sisters were looking worried. I excused myself, explaining I wanted to drive home, slowly, and look for her along the way. Sister Charlotte and Sister Margaret declared they would come along. It seemed smart to have two extra pairs of eyes.

We drove as slowly as traffic would allow, scanning both sides of the street, peering at every pedestrian on the long, long bridge over the Petrusse. No sign of Andrea; in fact, no sign of any child out walking alone. Or maybe she wasn't alone. I tried to dismiss that frightening possibility. I wound through downtown, so busy and bustling it was impossible to spot anyone. I pulled up at our house, now terribly concerned and at a loss for what to do. I immediately called Bob, who rushed home from the bank.

I asked our *au pair*, Nellie, if there had been any calls. She shook her head and joined our anxious circle. We had been waiting to call the police, hoping hard that Andrea would miraculously appear. The sisters recalled that the father of one of the kindergarten pupils was a state trooper and proposed calling him. We were debating what action to take, knowing that it was high time to do something for over an hour had passed, when the doorbell rang.

We all were frozen in place for a moment. The sisters, who were such a calming presence, began to pray even more fervently. I said a silent prayer. Nellie ran down the long flight of stairs to the vestibule and opened the heavy door. We heard voices coming back up and one was Andrea's! We rejoiced as she came into the living room, composed as could be.

"Momma, you were late!" admonished our independent little miss. "So I had to walk home," she concluded, obviously feeling completely justified in doing so.

We were much too relieved to reprimand her then and there and were overwhelmed at her ability to find her way home, through traffic and over such a distance. Later, I found a way to forestall any future straying. I was walking downtown one day with the children, who were, as usual, resisting my efforts to corral them, when we passed a prominent edifice that boasted a huge stone eagle perched atop the cornice. The outsized bird gave me an idea and, contrary to advice in every child-rearing book, I decided to scare the kids into compliance. Whenever they let go of my hand, or wanted to cross the street without holding on, or might contemplate running off when told to stay and wait, I would invoke the Eagle! The Eagle was always watching! The Eagle would swoop down and carry them off if they didn't follow my street commands! The scare tactic worked, at least for as long as I needed it to, and the kids weren't scarred.

Eventually, the days unfolded routinely. We entertained a lot, both our new local friends and those from the American community. Mid-week was the prime time to invite guests to dinner or give a party; it was also the time of choice for going out to the homes of others. This seemed strange at first, but it did reserve the weekend for family and excursions out of town, so it was a welcome change.

As time went by, I became concerned about the future school situation, for we now had two young children who would be starting school during our tour. I discovered that there was a school of sorts sponsored by the Goodyear facility there with classes that met at the plant, but I also learned that this arrangement wasn't satisfying the needs of the American community in and around Luxembourg City. Also, I knew the country was vitally interested in improving its industry by way of technology transfer, and attracting American know-how was an important part of its strategy. However, American workers were reluctant to move their families to Luxembourg for the one or two years of their stay because they feared their children would not be well enough prepared for their logical advancement once back in the States. I decided to find a satisfactory solution that would meet the needs of both constituencies involved, as well as my own.

The answer seemed clear, if daunting—establish a school with an American curriculum! I met with the parents of school-aged children and energized a PTA that endorsed the idea and voted its support. I enlisted the help of the heads of American companies in the area and we met with the Minister of Education of Luxembourg. The CEOs agreed to pay the tuition of their families' children and the Minister rented us a building for a dollar a year. I consulted with my sister, Marilyn, an elementary school teacher in Vermont, who gave me invaluable advice on texts and teaching methods.

We formed a board of directors, recruited and hired teachers, both local and from the States, and, in under a year, were able to open the American School of Luxembourg. Any student who wanted to follow an American curriculum was eligible to enroll. More American families came to Luxembourg and enrollment grew to over one hundred in just the first year. I served as chair of the board during the time we lived there and was gratified to learn, years later, that the school still exists.

To meet the required numbers for enrollment, we had to recruit every possible student and so it was that Robbie started kindergarten at age four. Albeit young, he thrived there and soon gained an enviable reputation among his peers for the tales he could tell.

At a holiday cocktail party, his teacher told me how Robbie would regale the class with stories he had heard his dad relay about his trips to Yugoslavia, London, and elsewhere. Methinks his teacher encouraged him in this.

The American School was housed in a spacious building in the city with plenty of dirt around the concrete playground. And the children loved playing in the dirt. After recess, they would wash their hands at the sinks in their classrooms and dry them on the pull-down linen towels next to the sinks. My daughter liked first grade very much and did very well, but the teacher told me she had a problem sitting still. This behavior was a recent development and troubling, but I soon discovered the reason for her squirming when I examined her during the night as the doctor had instructed—she had worms! The cure took a while and our whole family had to take the treatment. Meanwhile, I advised the teachers and parents of the problem and was determined that the school children wouldn't be re-infected. My daughter's teacher, though, was unconcerned; he said everyone gets worms and, in essence, it's to be expected.

"Not in this school," I assured him, and proceeded to enlist the aid of my husband's bank to supply paper towels and dispensers in each classroom.

They were duly installed and the linen rolls removed. But when I came to the school the next day to inspect, I was chased down the long hallway by a very angry woman brandishing a mean looking broom and shouting something, unflattering, I'm sure, in *Lëtzebuergesch*, the local patois that was a tongue-twisting mixture of German and French. What had I done to deserve this, I wondered? I soon found out.

I ducked into the principal's office and found him trying to calm

the janitor who was complaining that the substitution of paper towels was a gross insult to his wife who laundered the linen towels
and never before had her handiwork so demeaned. It took quite a
while to explain that the change did not reflect poorly upon the
washing and ironing skills of his wife but that the paper towels
were more hygienic. We did not discuss the matter of worms per se
and the janitor seemed satisfied that his wife's reputation was not
ruined, so if the crazy Americans wanted to waste money on paper
towels, well, that was their funeral.

Our pets of the period were cats, not dogs. There were several,
but mainly a beautiful Burmese christened "Burma" by the children. Burma was given to us by Peggy, a dear friend of mine, and
I accepted him gratefully. He was quite the curious one, too.
Burma liked nothing better that to creep out of the playroom windows on the fourth floor of our townhouse (it seemed he could
push them open) and walk around the ledge that bordered the
building, then proceed to pace along the ledges of the abutting
building. He would not come back in when called, of course. The
children would be frantic and I totally frustrated. Our only solution was to leave the windows open upstairs and hope for Burma's
return. Eventually, he would wander back in, none the worse for
the wear.

Luxembourg City was a lovely place to live and had the added
advantage of being close to Paris. I had an excellent excuse to
travel there every three months because the nearest periodontist
was located there and I needed regular treatment. Despite the
dreaded scaling of the teeth I would face, I relished these day
trips. I would board the train early in the morning, keep my

appointment with the periodontist, (who turned out to have been trained by my periodontist in Boston—another bit of serendipity) and then enjoy the rest of the day. I rewarded myself by lunching and browsing at the English book store where I could find books for us and the children, or shopping at Fauchon's, the "millionaires' supermarket," for specialty foods, especially the divine chocolates, and still have time to take in a museum or a movie. I saw *Last Tango in Paris* in Paris! Dinner aboard the train en route home was a perfect way to end the day.

Every Memorial Day, Bob, as the dean of the foreign banking corps, and I were invited to attend a ceremony at the American Military Cemetery at Hamm, just outside Luxembourg City, to honor the American dead who had fought at the Battle of the Bulge and were buried there. These 5000 graves, marked by white crosses, are arrayed on a grassy hillside surrounded by dense forest. They are regularly visited by the Luxemburgers who decorate them with flowers or small flags and many locals care for individual graves as an expression of their gratitude for the American sacrifice. Among the graves is that of General Patton, who had been killed in an auto accident in Germany one year after the war ended. The Memorial Day ceremony was always a moving occasion, saluted as well with a fly-over of planes from the nearby U.S. Air Force Base in Bitburg, Germany.

One of the most amazing events of our life in Luxembourg occurred when construction crews that were building a new road out of the City unearthed a long stretch of the Appian Way! The small settlement that became Luxembourg City was strategically situated at the crossroads of two important Roman routes, from Paris to Trier and from Metz to Aix-la-Chapelle and now, here lay revealed the preserved remains of that famous Way. Its reddish tiles with their chariot wheel ruts were still intact from the time early in the first century A.D. when Roman legions were intent on bringing all of Europe under Caesar's rule. This startling and historic discovery brought people from all over to see for themselves. Then, in a generous gesture, the government announced that residents could take home some of the tiles! I rushed to the site along with hundreds of others and managed to select some choice ones. I treasure these relics of the distant past as my own tangible connection to a civilization of centuries ago.

MANCHESTER-BY-THE-SEA, MASSACHUSETTS

Four years after our arrival, we left Luxembourg. Burma traveled back with us to our house in Manchester-by-the-Sea. While we were holed up in a motel waiting to move back in, Burma took sick. We found a vet in Hamilton but it was too late and the children's beloved cat died. I felt they needed another pet to ease the transition to life in the States and began a search for, yes, another cat, an animal easier to select on short notice than a dog. The *Manchester Cricket* had run an ad for kittens, and with paper in hand, I visited the litter. There was an adorable calico kitty that I was certain would fill the bill and I immediately plucked her out of the box and took her home.

The children were playing outside and I approached them, kitty in jacket pocket, in much like the manner my uncle brought my first puppy to me. I reached in my pocket and pulled out the little creature, saying, "Surprise!" Andrea was delighted and immediately took the kitty from me, exclaiming, "Surprise," just assuming that was the kitty's name. So, Surprise she became, but

Surprize would be spelled with a "z," Andrea declared. "Prizer" soon found her calling—she became a watch-cat. She would station herself atop an outcropping of ledge at the corner of our property and sit there, waiting and watching for the children to come up the hill after school, then usher them safely up the driveway. Surprize lived with us for years, accompanying us on our move to Toronto and returning with us to Manchester where sometime later she became very ill. We took her to the vet and hoped she would recover, but she did not. It was Andrea who drove her to the vet one last time. It was dear Surprize's final trip.

The seventies were heady years for the revitalized women's movement and I became heavily involved. I was appointed by then Governor Michael Dukakis to the state's first Governor's Commission on the Status of Women in 1976 and served as a Commissioner for four years. During that period, I chaired a committee on education. Under new laws of the state relating to gender discrimination, I was given the authority to meet with textbook publishers and review and recommend changes to elementary school texts in order to bring them into compliance. The fun part was taking Dick and Jane's mothers out of the kitchen and showing them climbing a telephone pole or sitting behind an authoritative-looking desk. As Commissioner, I also organized an economic literacy program for women and did a lot of public speaking as an advocate on issues of importance to women.

I enrolled in two courses at the Economics Learning Center of the University of Massachusetts in Boston, immersing myself in "The Economics of Discrimination" and "Political Economy." I had become an early member of the National Organization for Women (NOW) and joined the League of Women Voters as well. I hauled my infant daughter to all the meetings so I could nurse her right on time. I was the total activist and my devotion to the "cause" required masterful scheduling and prioritizing, but it was all worth it.

One day, however, I was late coming home from my "women's work" and found my two little urchins stranded outside our house, seated on a retaining wall, waiting, waiting for me! I felt awful. Never before had I not been at home when they returned from school, and I made sure it never happened again.

During the election campaign of 1976, I campaigned hard for the Equal Rights Amendment (ERA). I even dragooned Andrea, a sixth-grader by now, to hold up signs in support of the Amendment. She and a girl friend stood out in the cold and loyally waved the signs as parents drove up to the school to pick up their children. I spoke at the elementary school, too, about the ERA. I'm not sure how effective my message was for the assembled audience, but I do recall that my talk had totally embarrassed my son.

The ERA was originally written way back in 1921 by the suffragist Alice Paul and has been reintroduced in Congress every year since 1923. Congress finally passed the amendment in 1972 and set 1979 as a deadline for ratification by the states. By 1977, 35 states had ratified, and the push was on to reach the required 38 states. But opposition had grown and it became apparent that more time would be needed beyond the 1979 deadline to gain the three more states necessary for passage. So, in March, 1977, NOW sought an extension of the deadline.

In November, 1977, I was chosen as one of the 2000 delegates to the congressionally funded National Women's Conference in Houston, Texas. It was an exhilarating event and fired up all us feminists for the continuing fight ahead. In July, 1978, I went to

Washington, D.C. to walk in the March for Equality organized by NOW to pressure Congress to pass the deadline extension. Over 100,000 marchers assembled on the Mall, making this the largest march in feminist history, but, alas, I wasn't one of them. A frantic phone call had come from Bob telling me Andrea was sick and couldn't go to school and that he had an important meeting at the bank and couldn't stay home to take care of her. I flew back to Manchester and resumed my primary role—that of mother. It was so gratifying to learn in October that Congress did indeed extend the deadline—to the end of June, 1982. The rally had worked!

However, when that fateful, final date arrived, the ERA remained three states short of ratification. Supporters of the ERA all over the country had lobbied state legislatures, marched, rallied, petitioned, picketed, advertised, boycotted, and committed acts of civil disobedience in an enormous effort to win its passage. It was not enough. An analysis of the ERA vote compiled by the National Organization for Women for the four key targeted state legislatures, in Florida, Illinois, North Carolina and Oklahoma, showed that Republicans had deserted the ERA and Democratic support was not strong enough to pass the amendment. The analysis made clear that the single most obvious problem was the gender and racial imbalance in the legislatures: more than two thirds of the women, all of the African-Americans but less than fifty percent of the white men in the targeted legislatures cast pro-ERA votes in 1982.* If it weren't for all those unenlightened men, we would now have the ERA enshrined in the Constitution.

We fought the good fight and lost, but the amendment is not dead. It continues to be reintroduced in Congress and when three more states vote yes, the ERA could still become the 28th

---

*NOW Chronology of the Equal Rights Amendment, www.now.org/issues/eco-momic/cea/history.html

Amendment to the U.S. Constitution. Still, our efforts have not been in vain—young women nowadays are reaping the benefits of our hard work and there are major cracks in glass ceilings. We have won major battles, if not the war.

TORONTO, ONTARIO

The Bank of Boston Luxembourg proved successful and, when Ontario opened its doors to foreign banks, Bob was ready with a proposal that was approved for setting up Bank of Boston Canada. We moved to Toronto in 1982, to a handsome house in Rosedale, and enrolled the children in North Toronto Collegiate High School. Later, I returned to school as well—for an MBA at the Schulich School of Business at York University in Toronto.

One day not long after our arrival, I spotted an article in the *Globe and Mail* about a Doberman that had been rescued by the Humane Society and needed a home. The poor animal had been attacked and left for dead in a city park. The dog had undergone a ninety-minute operation to receive eighty-seven stitches to the head and back but was now in good health, the article stated, and was eligible for adoption by the right family. We went to see the dog and were deemed qualified to offer a suitable home since we knew the breed well and had owned Dobermans before. Thus Blitz was welcomed as a member of the family and he and Surprize gradually became tolerant of one another.

Wet, clumpy snow defined winter in Toronto. On one such typical night, the children and I sat down to eat at the kitchen table that was tucked into a cozy alcove and lit with a lamp hanging from above. Bob was away on business but Blitz joined us, curled up on the floor, close to our chairs. We were ready to enjoy a steak dinner so I dug out my shiny stainless steel steak knives. Just as Rob was brandishing his steak knife, Blitz suddenly leaped up and in a split second had sunk his teeth in Rob's right shoulder and then, with a deliberate movement, fastened onto Rob's upper arm.

My daughter and I jumped up, knocking over the table; everything on it, food, drink, glass and china, crashed and broke on the quarry-tiled floor. We screamed and, for what seemed like forever, stood paralyzed, simply staring at Rob's horrible plight. The dog was proceeding to work his way down the length of Rob's right arm. Against all conventional wisdom, I tried to pry Blitz's steel-strong jaws away from Rob, tried to get my fingers between the dog's teeth and my son's skin, something that proved impossible to do—and dangerous.

Rob was in terrible pain and bleeding from the lacerating bites. He was in shock, I was sure. In my panic, it came to me that he might never write or draw again—for he was right-handed and so artistically talented! Blitz relinquished Rob's arm but now had attacked his right thigh. Finally, some sense prevailed and I remembered that throwing cold water on an attacking animal could stop it. Andrea had waded through the mess on the floor and had come around to where I was standing. I yelled at her to fill the pot I cooked the potatoes in with cold water and throw it on Blitz. The dog was now at Rob's knee, but suddenly clamped his jaws back on Rob's arm. At last Andrea had the pot full and heaved the water at the dog's head. It stopped him cold!

With head soaking wet, Blitz immediately backed away from Rob and became a docile dog again just as quickly as he had become an attack animal. He seemed totally unaware of what had just happened and appeared his friendly self so I told Andrea to lead him down into the recreation room and then call the Humane Society to come get him. Blitz obediently followed her downstairs. Meanwhile, I grabbed a jacket, threw it around Rob's shoulders and hurried him out to the car. I was worried sick about the damage to his arm and what might have happened to the nerves in his hand and wanted to get him to the hospital fast. I did not want to wait for an ambulance.

We lived at one end of a one-way oval, close to a connecting street that led to the main road to Sunnybrook Hospital. I definitely was not going to drive all the way around the oval, as one should, and instead, turned out of the driveway in the direction of the connecting street, less than half a block away. Heavy, wet snow was falling, visibility was low, but there was no mistaking the headlights directly in front of me!

A taxi was coming up our street, the correct way, and our cars met, almost bumper to bumper. I skidded to a stop, leaped out of the car, and ran in front of the taxi, waving my arms like a wild woman. It was cold and in the glare of the headlights, I realized I had no coat on and was still wearing a bloody apron, wet with the water thrown at Blitz. I ran round to the driver's window, screaming, "Back up, back up! I've got to get to the hospital fast. My son is bleeding. Back up, please!"

If my words didn't convince the taxi driver, then my appearance must have. The expression on his face was one of fear—for himself. For all he knew, I was the one who injured my son and could well do him harm. He backed up all the way to the entrance to our street and I barreled on to the hospital, sliding at times on the slick surface.

I left the car in the emergency lane and rushed into the hospital with Rob. He was cold, injured, and scared. I was concerned that paperwork would take an eternity, but not so. This was, after all, Canada, with its universal health care coverage, and we were tended to without delay. Rob was whisked away from me and I was told to wait outside the treatment room. I sat, shivering, on a bench in a bleak, empty corridor hearing Rob's screams as his wounds were cleansed with peroxide. The doctor did tell me to expect that reaction, but I couldn't help crying, helpless as I was to comfort him and so worried about the outcome.

Finally, the doctor emerged to report the gruesome news that the dog bites had communicated, that is, the teeth had gone completely through the flesh and met. The better news was that it appeared that movement in his fingers was not compromised. There were about fourteen stitches to his arm, more on his leg, all crudely done since the doctors were inexperienced and used an old zig-zag method of sewing up the wounds. Later there were X-rays and then therapy for his hand, but, in time, thank goodness, Rob regained full use of his writing and drawing hand, though he still bears the scars of his ordeal.

Blitz had been picked up by the Humane Society by the time we returned home. Evidently, a glint of light off Rob's steak knife had caused the poor animal to snap and re-live the awful experience of when he had been assaulted—with a knife! We had not known those details of the dog's injuries and were sad to learn that now he would have to be put down.

The *Globe and Mail* had done an article about us and our admiration of the breed when we adopted Blitz. It had generated a lot of local interest among our neighbors and Rob's high school friends as well, so when he showed up in class the week after the attack, he felt the story had by now made him look pretty stupid but the kids thought it was hilarious to see him in stitches.

We didn't stay dogless for long. Sieger, another handsome red and tan Doberman, soon became our next pet. He was a stable, good natured, affectionate Dobe and quite playful. He loved to run and we often took him to exercise at a nearby park. One day, he took off on his own, frolicking down our street in a direction that would take him to a major artery. Rob went racing after him. It was like chasing the gingerbread man, Rob said, for it seemed Sieger was saying, "Catch me if you can," as he ran on and on. Finally, dodging traffic and almost out of breath, Rob caught up with him before he could run out on Mt. Pleasant Avenue. Sieger was saved!

Sieger returned with us to Manchester when we moved back from Toronto. He remained a dear, devoted member of our family for years. Eventually, the children left home and Bob and I divorced. It was difficult for Bob to keep the dog at the house and I couldn't take him to my apartment. We found a retirement home for Dobermans in New Hampshire and, before I left Manchester for the last time, I drove Sieger there. He would be taken care of for as long as he lived, I was assured.

It was so very hard to leave him, the more so because, like our dog days, our marriage was also over.

The newly minted college graduate of Washington
University, St. Louis, Missouri, June 1950. Photo by
Marie Hendricks.

At the station in Upper Alton, IL, bound for
Washington, D.C. Summer 1951. Photo by Marie
Hendricks.

Sailing away aboard the SS *United States*,
September 1952.

Shipmates Clem (left) and Otto.

1.262114 ✳
/448

OCCUPATIONAL FORCE TRAVEL PERMIT
LAISSEZ-PASSER DES FORCES D'OCCUPATION
Пропуск для оккупационных войск

Ширлей Мари Х Е Н Д Р И К С

SHIRLEY MARIE HENDRICKS

(Name, nom, имя и фамилия)

DA Civ /гражд. США PP# 66531

(Rank, Grade, чин)   (Army No., Numéro Matricule, и удосто-
                         верения личность)

Hq VMP /служ. при ОСФА

(Organization, Unité ou Service, организация)

is authorized to travel from
est autorisé(e) à voyager de   Vienna Austria
имеет право ездить из
                               Вены, Австрии

to British Zone Austria   and return.
à   et retour.
                                                 и обратно.
брит. зону чер с ов. зону чер Земмеринг
Restrictions or limitations if any   Via Semmering
Restrictions ou limitations eventuelles
Имеются ли какие нибудь ограничения   By rail or Auto

                               поездом или автомашиной

Shirley M. Hendricks

(Signature of Bearer, Signature du titulaire, подпись владельца)

Travel permit for entering the Soviet Zone of Austria.

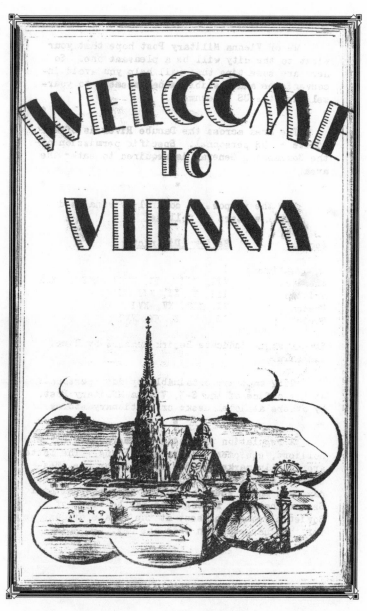

U.S. Army orientation brochure supplied to Sgt. Robert Perry.

Right: Vienna's famous *Riesenrad* in the Prater, June 1953.

Below: American band at the Changing of the Guard ceremonies, Vienna, September 1952. Photo by R.S. Perry.

Changing of the Guard ceremonies, Vienna, September 1953:

Top: A platoon of Russian soldiers.

Bottom: The Soviet Army Band. Photos by R.S. Perry.

Aboard "California" the camel, at the Pyramids, Egypt, April 1953.

"I dreamed I went to a Halloween party in my Maidenform bra!" With Bob, Vienna, October 1953.

WEINSCHENKE ZUM DRITTEN MANN
Toni Karas
AUSTRIA   WIEN   VIENNA

These three musicians serenaded us upon our engagement, Vienna, December 1953.

Our MG-TD in British racing green, Vienna, 1954. Photo by R.S. Perry.

Right: Mr. and Mrs. Robert S. Perry at our reception in the Hotel Sacher, Vienna, March 6, 1954. Photo by Simonis.

Left: The Bride can bake!

Strolling musicians in a wine garden in Grinzing, Vienna. Photos by R.S. Perry.

With Hasso in Perlacher Forest, Munich,
1960. Photo by R.S. Perry.

Hasso at home in Munich, Fall 1959. Photo by R.S. Perry.

Off to a Fasching party,
Munich, February 1960.
Photo by R.S. Perry.

The Hendrickses and Perrys before setting sail for Europe aboard the SS *America*,
September 1962. Photo by William Hartley.

Left: Baron and I dressed up for Christmas, 1963, Grünwald/Munich. Photo by R.S. Perry.

Below: The Americans in Munich (AIM) Club rafting down the Isar River, Munich, 1964.

Andrea with her Grandpa George and Baron, Charlottesville, Virginia, June 1968.

View of our townhouse in Luxembourg City from the Stadtpark across the street, 1970. Photo by R.S. Perry.

Left: Andrea and Robbie at home in Luxembourg City, March 1973. Photo by R.S. Perry.

Right: Sieger guards the door to the house, Toronto, 1982. Photo by R.S. Perry.

Chekhov grave site (*right*) and Khrushchev's final resting place (*bottom*) in the cemetery at the Novodevichy Monastery, Moscow 1993.

In costume as Arkadina in "The Sea Gull," Boston, Spring 1992.

3

Sentimental Me

Gonna take a sentimental
journey to renew old memories...
—Ben Homer, Bud Green, and Les Brown

*I*t was my seasonal mantra: when the temperature drops into the 40s, it's high time to switch wardrobes. I would be late doing it if the weather had been mild, but also because I've always found this task quite a chore. Twice a year, the fall and winter clothes had to replace the spring/summer wardrobes and vice versa. When the children were home and we lived in a large house, I would empty all the closets and cart the off-season outfits into the attic, then lug down all the clothing that was waiting to be worn currently and arrange it in everyone's closet.

The change-over process also involved considerable weeding out, although it seemed the children actually required new clothes every season, at least until they were full-grown. Back then there were groans of protest at the sight of something "too gross" to be seen in again. Sometimes, a certain number was warmly welcomed once more and happily worn. Now, I greet my recycled clothes like old friends and am most reluctant to part with any of them, even if they have gone out of fashion.

That feeling of attachment made it all the more difficult to pare down my wardrobe when I was preparing to move from Manchester to Boston, leaving a house, a husband, a long chapter of my life. But everything wouldn't fit in the limited space in my new apartment. So out of the closet came the clothes and their ghosts with them. Goodbye to that red pants suit, a lovely gift from my husband one Christmas and a one-time favorite, though now outmoded. Farewell to the designer dress, in pink, that I bought during our visit to London one year—I still liked it but it really was too unfashionable. So many of my outfits were incompatible with the present styles. Incompatible—just like the two of us had become. Incompatible, yet finding the parting hard to do. It was not that love was out of style, it was just that we were out of synch.

But divorce decisions had been made and, finally, wardrobe decisions as well. The pile of castoffs, all wearable still, made a substantial contribution to the Salvation Army. Nonetheless, I still moved with too many clothes. Why couldn't I have been more ruthless in my weeding out? Some things were classic, some things I just liked too much, some I thought would come back into fashion, but some things simply had too many memories attached to them.

Every season, I still go through my closet and find I am parting with fewer and fewer pieces. True, I am buying fewer new clothes, but I should be able to cull, especially since it would yield up more space and everything would be less crowded together. Yet I am not able to. Just like I found it hard to clean out my storage unit when the time came to leave Boston. My childhood toys, books, heirloom linens, old telephones...I've kept them all for all have meaning for me.

Like my "interview suit" or the gown I wore to the Maple Leaf Ball, all these stored treasures take me on a sentimental journey, connect me with stored memories, some of which I might never recall were there not such tangible triggers. Once, when putting away my bicycle for the winter, I had to move the crank-handled telephone that had been in our family home in Illinois. As soon as I saw it, I thought about our party line, and how the phone would ring through to "Central"—a home-based operator who listened in on everyone's calls, but who could be an invaluable resource in emergency situations—she was an early "9-1-1."

I could see myself again, getting more and more frustrated trying to reach Central, what with the scratchy connection and the feeling that my conversation was being monitored and would soon circulate around town. It was my father who finally rescued us all by forming a small local phone company and installing cradle phones and private line service in our community. He even strung the wires and kept the books as treasurer. I still have that old black 1950s cradle phone, too.

My father could do most anything. He understood engines, machines, telephones, telegraphy, and knew Morse code. He was a fine carpenter and gardener, and played the saxophone. He had once worked for the New York Central railroad and had a passion for trains so he was our authority on rail travel and made all the arrangements for my departure, after college, for Washington, D.C. and my new job with the Central Intelligence Agency. We all went to the train station in Upper Alton to see me off that hot

August day—Mother, Dad, my sister, and her boyfriend, Bill. Dad
had arranged to have my trunk sent ahead, by rail, so I was carrying only an overnight case. I was to change trains in St. Louis and
take a Pullman on to Washington.

After our teary good-byes on the platform, for I didn't know
when I would see my family again, Dad came aboard with me to
make sure I found the right seat. He put my case up on the over-
head shelf and instructed me once again on how to change trains.
I remember being very sad, despite my excitement, and glad to
have Dad with me as long as possible. I knew he had conflicting
feelings about my leaving.

"I'm so proud of you, Shirley, for having landed this job with
the CIA, but I'm worried about you—living in a big city and being
so far away," Dad said slowly.

Then, "Take good care of yourself," he counseled, "and be sure to
write."

"Oh, I will, Daddy, I will," I assured him, and tried to smile.

He kissed me goodbye, but hesitated to leave. "I have something for you, for the trip."

Out of his pocket he fished a shiny, collapsible cup made of
aluminum. It was topped with a lid decorated with sailboats.
"This should come in handy," he explained, handing it to me. His
giving me this was so very special because Dad himself had never
before actually bought something for me; mother was always the
buyer of our gifts. And it was so very thoughtful, too. For if one
had a cup at hand, she would be able to get a drink of water from
any tap or fill it from a drinking fountain and swallow standing
up, a much more satisfactory stance than bending over and getting one's hair wet in the process.

I was so touched by this tender, simple gesture and the love for me it conveyed. We had a last, long hug and then Dad was gone. I was on my own. My eyes were full of tears and I held on to the cup all the way to St. Louis. It was like taking a part of him with me and it comforted me.

I was immensely cheered at the sight of my dear friend, my sorority sister BB, who came to Union Station to see me off. Following Dad's instructions, I had no problem finding the sleeping car and BB came on board to help me get settled in my compartment. She, too, had a goodbye gift for me—a small cosmetic case that accompanied me on many another journey and never failed to remind me of my far-away friend. The conductor's call of "All aboard!" abruptly ended our short time together and then BB was gone as well.

I took the cup with me to Europe and, later, on business trips and other journeys, both for sentimental reasons and just in case I might need it. It came with me on my move from Boston to Oxford, Mississippi. It now sits on a kitchen shelf, replaced by bottled water but not replaced in my heart.

I suppose my sentimental self needs all these reminders that have the power to engender so many trains of thought. My sentimental self, it seems, won't let me let go and has made me into something of a pack rat. Yet I'm not a saver for saving's sake. Everything I keep is by choice because of a special association it evokes. Everything I keep keeps my memory bank full and enriches my life and this way I know I shall never be overdrawn.

4

What's a Woman to Do?

> *If at first you don't succeed try, try again.*
> —Thomas H. Palmer

C ity life! I loved it. My apartment was just minutes from where I worked at the Canadian Consulate General, located in the Prudential Center in Boston. I could walk over in eight minutes. No more getting up at 6:00 a.m. and enduring the tardy train ride in from the North Shore.

I loved my job, too. As the senior political and economic officer at the Consulate and aide to the Consul General, I served as an advocate for Canada's positions on matters of bilateral interest. We lobbied the New England Congressional delegation on such issues, one of the most important at the time being the matter of free trade between Canada and the United States, an effort that culminated successfully in the Free Trade Agreement that entered into effect in January of 1989. The Consulate also advocated the reduction of acid rain pollutants and after years of courting a reluctant U.S., Canada was finally able to sign an Acid Rain Accord between the two countries in 1991.

So things were good. Everything except my social life, that is. What's a woman to do about that? I had to remedy the situation. I didn't know many people in the city except for my colleagues at work. I'd have to look elsewhere for after-hours company. I'd read about an agency that paired singles according to their common interests with the help of a computer. That seemed as good a basis as any for meeting someone who liked to do the same things I did so I filled out an endless form that recorded all my likes and dislikes on just about everything. In a sort of summary, I was asked to list the three things I most liked doing and came up with going to museums, to the movies, and dining out. Then, I was to list the three activities I most disliked. OK: dog races, bowling, and stock car races. Surely there wasn't anyone who would hit that trifecta. Then, I had to indicate what kind of work I would like this ideal person to do. I picked "professional."

It didn't take long for a letter from the agency to arrive bearing word of the perfect match for me. Presumably this man would want to do things I enjoyed so I was astounded to read that he loved dog races and bowling and hated going to museums and movies! And he worked at a post office. Was this complete inversion of my preferences some kind of a joke, I wondered? I phoned the agency. No indeed, it wasn't a joke; this was the result of the agency's highly touted computer match program that evidently backfired. It took a while, but I got my money back.

Undeterred, I turned to the personal ads. "Tall, Gary Cooper look-alike who enjoys eating out" seemed promising. When he walked into the lobby of my apartment building I saw that his description was half right. He was tall. Similarities to the movie star ended with his height. But I was hungry and at least looked forward to dinner. He recommended a Mexican restaurant within walking distance. I liked Mexican food, although he didn't bother to ask. After we were seated there and the waiter approached with menus, Gary Cooper waved them away.

"Oh, we won't need menus. We'll have the specials you advertise here on this coupon!" Cooper gave it to the waiter with a triumphant flourish.

I couldn't see what was on offer, and was evidently captive to Cooper's coupon as I watched the waiter scribble down the request. Then the waiter asked if we would like a drink. Cooper said he would like a glass of water, "But from the tap, not any of that bottled stuff," he instructed.

I ordered a Dewars and soda, realizing I would need some fortification to get through the meal.

"No, no. Cancel that," Cooper cried. "It's not covered by the coupon!"

"No, bring it," I challenged, "and I'll pay for it." I sounded as sarcastic as possible but Cooper was unfazed. What a clod; he hadn't a clue. I debated whether to stay because this contretemps was a real conversation stopper and I had lost my appetite—both for food and for him. I downed my drink, plunked down some dollars, and dashed.

Surely that encounter was just bad luck, I rationalized, and after a time I got my nerve up to go back to reading the personals. One stood out. This man worked in the science building at Harvard and was able to meet at a restaurant in a hotel in Cambridge that was on the T's red line. I described what I looked like and would be wearing. I should have waited in the gift shop so I could have scouted the scene and scooted out the other door, but there I sat, in the lobby, totally identifiable and available. Hadn't I remembered anything from my spy days? It was warm day, but rainy, and the man of the ad wore a raincoat that hit him above the knees. He looked rough, not at all how I envisioned the professor type I was expecting. He made a bee-line for me.

I managed a polite greeting and we headed for the restaurant. As soon as we reached a table, the waiter asked to take our coats. Under his raincoat, the Harvard man wore a shirt with short sleeves rolled up to display his muscular, ornate arms, both of which were festooned with creatures of the sea and a couple of anchors. The waiter rolled his eyes; I couldn't stop staring.

"I was in the Navy," he explained.

"I see." I swallowed hard. "And what do you do now?" I ventured, dreading the answer.

"Oh, I'm the janitor in the science building at Harvard."

I couldn't help looking stunned. "Look," Tattoo-Man said. "I guess I sort of misled you, but I'd like to stay and buy you lunch."

I just couldn't waltz out; after all, I had gotten myself into this by not asking more questions, by making assumptions, and he seemed genuinely sorry he hadn't been more forthcoming, so I stayed. Tattoo-Man entertained me with tales of his nautical adventures and we parted amicably. Next time, if there is a next time, I vowed to take precautions—and use the lessons I had learned.

There was a next time, much later. The third time is a charm, so I believed, and proceeded to contact a "professional man seeking woman who enjoys the arts, fine cuisine, and classical movies." My winning combination! How could I resist? I set up a meeting in front of a small café in the Back Bay and asked him to describe himself so I could identify him. I told him I would find him; he wouldn't have to worry about finding me. I knew the café and arrived a half-hour early. I checked out the back door to make sure it was unlocked, then stationed myself inside at a table near the rear from which I had an unobstructed view of the front.

Right on time, a figure appeared outside. He stood in one spot for a short while then began to walk back and forth. That's the guy, I was sure. He fit his own description—tall, large boned, and blessed with a full head of hair. Indeed he was tall, large too. And there was lots of hair, but it was on top of the biggest head I had ever seen—a head out of all proportion even to his big body. I had to get a better look at his face. I moved toward the front of the café, stopping at the counter as if contemplating a choice among the muffins, and glanced outside.

He looked like...like The Beast! Yes, that was it. His face was utterly unattractive—ugly, in fact—and his huge head atop the hulking shoulders reminded me of nothing other than that poor creature in the tale of "Beauty and the Beast." I gasped at the eerie resemblance. No matter how nice he might have been, I couldn't bear to meet him. "Beauty" had to flee and fortunately, she knew her way out.

The best laid plans certainly went awry for me. I had three strikes and was definitely out. So I decided just to go about my business and not too long after that last unsuccessful incident, at a conference I attended, I met a great guy—by chance. So much for planning and perusing the personals!

5

Vienna Revisited

Wien, Wien, nur du allein
Sollst stets die Staat meiner Traume sein
—Dr. Rudolf Sieczynski

*A*h, Vienna, Vienna, you shall always be the only city of my dreams, and yes, you are the city where I was the luckiest and happiest, as the lyrics of the lovely song confess. You were the glamorous, glittering capital of my imagination, the Eastern-edged city of Western culture. The place of palaces, waltzes, elegance, and art. I dreamed of dancing in your ballrooms, walking in your woods, cruising along your shores on the beautiful, blue Danube.

Then, when you became real for me, you had changed. You became the outpost for the Allies, a city set many miles within the Soviet zone of occupied Austria. Your skies were gray, your lights were dim, your buildings scarred, your economy shaky, your people, overly polite as always, were now welcoming Americans. And we came. To protect and aid you, and to spy. For within your international city limits, you were home to refugees, defectors, dissidents, and, most significant of all, representatives of the intelligence services of all the Cold War countries.

That is how I found you, Vienna, struggling to overcome the recent past and chock-full of present intrigue. There, amid your old landmarks and reviving traditions, in your reopened opera houses, in your wine gardens and cafés, in the Stadtpark, I discovered that city of my dreams, albeit a rather tarnished version. Still, this image was burnished by the glamour of conspiracy, the excitement of espionage with its whiff of danger that combined to make you relevant and real as well as eternally enchanting to me.

I would stroll in your lovely *Stadtpark* in spring, stopping to smell the beautiful lilacs bursting from their bushes, and in summer, marveling at the roses that seemed to be blooming everywhere, blessing the benches full of Viennese who took the time to rest and enjoy the heavenly scents of the season. I enjoyed drinking the new wine at the *Heurige*, the wine taverns in Grinzing, despite the horrible headaches one was bound to suffer the next day. I loved singing along with the strolling musicians as they played their *Schrammelmusik*, those sentimental Viennese favorites everyone knew by heart—I always requested *"Sag beim Abschied leise Servus,"* believing in the song's promise that soon after parting there would come a gentle greeting.

On weekends, I would sip espresso in your *Kaffeehäuser*, where time was of no consequence and the locals could nurse a large cup, always served with a small glass of water on a tray, all afternoon, while reading newspapers affixed to their wooden poles and smoking smelly *Galoise* cigarettes. I would treat myself to some fattening and fabulous pastry at Demel's. Along with crowds of Viennese, I would buy *Stehplatz* tickets to the *Volksoper* for a pittance and stand enchanted all through Wagner or Verdi or Strauss. This was indeed the old world, the alt Wien of which I'd read and dreamed.

This was also the Cold War world in which I was living. I would walk the narrow streets and wide boulevards on surveillance assignments or jump on and off streetcars after my target, cover colleagues at their café meetings; monitor agent meetings in our safe houses and always watch to see if I were being followed. So many locations became familiar for these secret reasons, but were nonetheless interesting and popular places I vowed one day to revisit. There were also places I could not go.

We with the Central Intelligence Agency were forbidden to travel into the Soviet sector of the city. However, on Fridays, boyfriend Bob would take me to a Czech restaurant located on the edge of the Soviet sector and next door to the Soviet motor pool. There, at sunset, the soldiers would assemble to lower their flag and then sing for at least half an hour! What a moving chorus they made, singing with great feeling their soulful Russian songs. We would devour our tasty *chivapchachi* or *shish kebob*, down our Pilsner beer and listen quietly to this unique serenade. I often wondered if the soldiers were aware of our presence and, if so, could understand our appreciation of those moments of man's humanity that erased our differences through the common language of song.

Oh, how important all we cold-warriors were! How important I was, too! How young and inspired. How young and pretty. How young! And so excited at getting married in the city of my dreams.

We held our wedding reception here at the Hotel Sacher where I sit now, sipping a Scotch and soda, seeing again in my mind's eye all those assembled to wish us well on that cold March day of many years ago. There I am, warm in my white velvet gown, cutting the cake and finding to my satisfaction that it was indeed a white cake, not the famous Sacher torte, underneath the white icing! There we are early the next day, Mr. And Mrs. Robert Perry, sneaking to the *Bahnhof* to catch the military train out of the Soviet zone, for we were married in the midst of a security ban on travel and were ordered to ride in the courier compartment of the "Mozart," as the American train was affectionately known. Above all, we were told to depart as unobtrusively as possible. I can evoke again the consternation we experienced upon encountering the same crew of celebrating friends and co-workers who had been at our wedding as they came marching along the platform, showering us with rice and singing loudly to the strains of the oompah band they had hired to see us off. So much for sneaking away.

Ah, memories. How selective they are. They are playing out in the theatre of my mind, all out of order, independent of my attempts to conjure them up in sequence.

"*Danke, Herr Ober*," I say to the waiter, refusing another drink.

I just want to lean back and savor whatever the next episode will be. I close my eyes and it begins. I am leaving the villa way out in the 19th *Bizirk* that I share with my girl friend and colleague. It's my birthday, a rainy January evening, and I am eager to get downtown to the *Musikveriensaal* where I shall meet my date for the *Opernball*, the most exclusive event of the re-established social season, held during *Fasching,* at which debutantes make their bows to society. I am resplendent in an ankle length, full-skirted, red silk dress with a becoming off-the-shoulder neckline—the only formal thing I had to wear—and I worry that I might contrast too wildly with the white gowned women.

The ancient taxi is waiting. I see myself dashing outside, slipping on the wet walkway and falling into a snowbank in my haste. I am rescued immediately through the combined efforts of the cab driver, my landlord, and the local *gendarme* who was slogging through the snowbanked sidewalks just in time. We all brush me off and no great harm is done, except now I am throughly chilled.

Like the old streetcars that were shipped from New York City to run on Vienna's tracks, the cabs come from elsewhere, too—from London. Wheels from the West! Just so they get me there, thought I, as I stumble inside where it seems to be still raining. I ask the driver to roll up his window but he couldn't, he says.

"Sehen Sie, Fraülein, haben wir hier eine 'Peutet'rl.'"

"A what?" I exclaim, mystified.

He patiently explains: the windshield wiper no longer worked reliably—perhaps it would go and perhaps it wouldn't. So he has to reach outside and move it back and forth by hand and that means he has to leave the window down. Obviously, this made sense, so I huddle in the opposite corner of the clammy back seat wishing myself already at the ball.

Then, as if in defense of Vienna's entire transportation system, the taxi driver proudly proclaims, *"Manchesmal, haben wir eine 'Tourjour'tl,'"* and this kind of wiper, he declares, works all the time. What a descriptive blending of the Austrian penchant both for the French word and the use of the diminutive. The two expressions have been a staple of my vocabulary ever since, defining ever so accurately the unpredictable workings of the many instruments we handle everyday.

Finally I arrive, not too much the worse for wear, and meet my escort. We watch the entrance of the Chancellor of Austria and many of his cabinet and other notables, all resplendent in formal dress *mit ordens*, impressive medals and decorations, as they pass through the avenue formed by the debutantes and their escorts. Between dances and glances, I observe the wealth and left-over royalty of Vienna. The big beer baron, complete with mutton chops and white tie, impresses me most as he holds court from his box, one of the luxurious loges that rings the floor. Every *Saal* in the huge building is festively decorated, buffet tables groan with fancy fares, waiters actually bustle and the famous Philharmonic strikes up its three-quarter-time tunes.

My date and I waltz the night away and, around 5:00 a.m., grab one of the hundreds of taxis that have gathered to whisk away the revelers. We are bound for a local late-night eatery to greedily gobble up a *Kater Frühstück*, the traditional hangover breakfast of goulash soup. The Cinderella evening is over, but the memory of it lingers on.

My mental curtain comes down. I open my eyes. I should leave the bar to meet my new love, but I am reluctant to leave my reveries. Amid the *"Kuss die Hand"* sendoffs from the bar, I decide to walk to the hotel where he and I are to rendezvous. There is still time to wander along the way. I begin to think of another time I returned to Vienna since those days behind the Iron Curtain. It was with my small daughter when I accompanied my husband on a business trip. We had stayed at the Hotel Imperial, the former Soviet headquarters, finally restored to its original splendor. It was a sumptuous experience. Vienna was once more beautiful and bustling. Yet places of personal importance that I showed my daughter—the church where I was wed, the city apartment where I had lived—were unchanged.

Walking along, I remember the apartment in the Skodagasse I

moved to when my roommate was transferred to Salzburg, safely inside the American zone. I see once again the large living room, encased in red velvet drapery, with the grand piano, a Bosendorfer, the best, that sat in the middle of the room. I mentally roam through the spacious dining room and the bedroom, then the kitchen and bath that I shared with the fascinating Czech landlady, Frau Hildegarde Josipovich, who kept a room of her own in the flat where she entertained her gentleman caller every Thursday afternoon at tea and on into the evening.

She was a handsome woman, statuesque, elegantly coiffed and dressed, and so very kind. She was for me *in loco parentis*, always solicitous of my well being, nursing me to recovery after my tonsillectomy with her special "snow pudding," playing the grand piano to cheer me when I felt homesick or despaired of the gray days. Thinking back, I remember how I would huddle, bundled in a blanket, near the tiled stove in the dining room on cold nights, and come spring, fling open the huge windows, sans screens, to inhale the fresh air. Suddenly, I hear again that band come to serenade the Socialist mayor, who lived at the same address, early on the first day of May.

I must hurry on. I sense that while I am not quite lost, I am confused. Things look—rearranged. My circuitous route takes me past a grand old *Apothetke* designed in the Art Nouveau style. I always liked the smell of the old fashioned apothecaries, where the scents of colognes, soaps, phosphate, and medicines co-mingle. I feel compelled to go in. Here time has stood still. Here the familiar looking clerks wear the same white coats and the same stolid, serious expressions. As always, everything is out of reach of the customer. I approach a long glass case— the main counter.

"*Was wünchen Sie, genedige Frau?*" the somber face inquires. I stand there, silent. Indeed, what do I want?

"Excuse me, I forgot what I came for," I finally reply, and make my retreat.

Perhaps I truly did forget what I came to Vienna for—or did I ever really know why? Ostensibly, it was to meet my boyfriend and logistically, it made sense. He was living in Europe so Vienna was an easy trip for him. And I know the city, I reasoned; I could show him around; I could speak the language, facilitate our stay. It would be great to be back and revisit my old haunts. But beyond all that, what did I hope to find? How did I think I would react, being again in this beloved city, so changed now, and so charged with personal and private memories? Was I trying to re-create the past? I am increasingly unsure, but I am beginning to understand that I, too, have changed, so how could I see the city through the same eyes? Older now and mature, divorced from the man I married here as well from that young woman who first discovered Vienna, and long since out of the spy business, I am almost new to you, *liebe Wien*, just as you seem new to me.

I meet my man, and it is wonderful to see him again. We dine at my old favorite restaurants—the Balkan Grill, the Drei Husaren, the Feuervogel—all still popular with the tourists. We promenade on the fashionable *Kärntner Strasse,* now so bustling, looking a lot like 5th Avenue and proudly displaying New York prices as well. We see *Die Fledermaus* in the gorgeous, renovated Opera House, my first visit there ever. Late on a damp winter afternoon, we walk around the deserted Prater, Vienna's amusement park nestled in the shadow of the great *Riesenrad*, the renown giant ferris wheel with swinging boxcars for seats. I used to love coming here. Suddenly, out of the corner of my mind's eye I see Orson Wells running through the Prater in the dark. I hear a zither somewhere strumming the unmistakable theme from "The Third Man." My memories are haunting me, the past is pursuing me.

It follows me through the Bellvedere museum where my boyfriend and I gaze together at Klimt's "The Kiss" and I recall the thrill of seeing that spectacular painting for the first time, with my husband. The past confuses me now and I lose my way in a tangle of side streets as we go in search of the Boheme Bar in the Dorotheergasse, the smartest bar in Vienna back when and now perhaps no longer there. It tricks me on the way to Grinzing to drink again that district's well known wine. The surroundings seem so very different; even streets have been re-routed. And when we finally arrive at a *Heurigen*, there are no longer the strolling musicians, the accordian player and violinist, the pair who always used to sing, "*Adieu, mein kleiner Gardeoffizier, adieu. Und vergiss mich nicht.*" At last, we wind our way back to our small hotel in the Grund, where we push together the wooden-framed beds and celebrate our reunion, blending like the golden couple of "The Kiss" in their erotic embrace.

This is a lovely interlude but short-lived for at last I recognize what is happening. My remembrances of this special place are tied inexorably to those treasured times of long ago when I first found you, Vienna, when I was young and every experience was exciting and fresh, when I met and married my first love. That past has captured me now and will neither let me relive those days gone by nor savor the present, hard as I try. I must leave and let it be. And so I bid adieu to you, *Liebling*, my new love, *und vergessen mich nicht*. And adieu to you, *alt Wien*. I shall never forget you, but I know I shall never see you again, nor need to. For you will always be that shimmering city of my young dreams and live on in my bittersweet memories.

6

The Maid of Moro Goes to Moscow

My favorite thing is to go where I've never been.
—Diane Arbus

*E*very day I waited for the postcard to arrive. I was anxious about my semester grade in Dramatics 431. Professor Carson would send it, on the postcard I addressed, embedded in a clue for me to decipher. I hoped to discover an A. Finally, the card arrived bearing the message, "For your grade, take the first letter of the name of a town about ten miles west of Moro, on the C&A railroad line." That had to be the city of Alton, on the rail line to Chicago. And that meant an A! Hurray!

Professor Carson was my drama teacher at Washington University in St. Louis. A kindly, humorous man who displayed infinite patience when putting us budding thespians through our paces in plays he directed and in the classroom where he introduced us to the literature of the stage. His courses attracted a small band of students whom he regarded as his charges and had great affection for, a feeling we reciprocated. In fact, he selected soubriquets for some of us, which is how I was dubbed the "Maid of Moro." Granted, I was from the little town of Moro, Illinois, and truly a maid, an unsophisticated sophomore in the big city, but did this nickname allude to a destiny at some future, fiery stake such as befell that famous maid of long ago? No, I decided, it was merely an alliterative appellation, something the professor delighted in creating. So I was safe to pursue my interests wherever they might lead. Maybe that would be the theater.

After all, I had trod the boards at a very early age and loved it. Only three, I had the title role in a Moro PTA production of "Little Star" at the town's elementary school. I can still recall the excitement of waiting in the wings, that is, in the coat room connected to the stage, redolent with smells of wet wraps and leftover lunches, and watching with the rest of the crowded-in cast for my cue and then, prompted by my mother, making my entrance! I walked past the blinding footlights, all the way over to stage left to where "Doc" Riggs, my character's father, sat, despondent, and then saying my lines written to cheer him up.

After this stellar debut there came, in time, elocution lessons from my mother. "Make nice motions, girls," she would instruct my sister and me, and we would comply, using arms and hands to accentuate nearly every action and emotion in the monologues we memorized. We gave recitations to relatives and church groups. At Alton high school, I tried out for and performed in just about every Dramatic Club play.

As a freshman at Washington University in St. Louis, I landed a leading role in the "Quad Show," a student revue. As a sophomore,

I played Juliet in a production of *Romeo and Juliet* sponsored by the drama guild at nearby Concordia Seminary. I've forgotten my Romeo but Montague was the young seminarian Martin Marty. A Lutheran minister, Rev. Marty became a distinguished professor emeritus at the University of Chicago Divinity School and is one of the foremost commentators on American religious life and culture.

Another interesting association surrounds the play. It was reviewed by my English professor, William Inge, who was also the drama critic for the St. Louis newspaper, *The Star Times*. I'd earned an A in composition in his English 101 class but was far more impressed with his favorable account of my performance. This bolstered my acting aspirations coming as it did from a budding playwright for it was at WU that Inge wrote the first draft of his play, "Come Back, Little Sheba," using as its working title, "Front Porch." I went on to major in drama and English, taking part in every production I could. My thespian skills were well honed.

But after graduation, it wasn't Broadway that beckoned; it was Washington. I had received a graduate fellowship from the university and was half-heartedly studying for a master's degree in counseling and personnel. But I needed a part-time job to supplement my stipend and went one day to the student employment office to scan the bulletin board for leads. What I found was a cryptic notice saying a government agency was looking for recent college graduates to work in Washington and abroad! What an antidote for boredom such a job would be!

"Tell me about this position, please," I all but demanded of Mrs. Settle, the startled director of the employment office.

"Well, dear, I can't tell you much," she replied, "but here are some forms to fill out and send in and then you'll find out all you need to know." The forms were to be sent to the Central Intelligence Agency in Washington, D.C.!

It seemed to take forever to fill out the multi-paged personal history statement and three months more for my clearance to come through—three hot, long summer months of anxious waiting, at home, for I had quit the graduate program to begin assembling my belongings, all of which fit into one large trunk. Finally the trunk and I were off to Washington, DC, via the same rail line Professor Carson cited, only now it was the GM&O. A year later, the CIA sent the trunk and me to Europe. My amateur theatrics went on hold for the duration of my service with the agency and again while I concentrated on being a wife and mother.

One Thanksgiving time, years later, when living alone in Boston, I boarded another train, the Amtrak, en route to Philadelphia to visit my daughter. The train was packed with people but I managed to get a seat by a window; however, it soon became apparent that I couldn't stay there. The cold November air seeped in around the window and the heat was tepid at best. I was so cold! I glanced at my seat mate, a man who looked like he would be comfortable in any seat, bundled up as he was, and rationalized that, after all, pantyhose didn't offer the same protection that trousers did.

"Excuse me, but would you mind changing seats with me?" I inquired.

He smiled his agreement. We switched seats and then began a conversation that quickly revealed his interest, and mine, in the theater. In fact, he was planning to direct Chekhov's *The Sea Gull* for The Fenway Players, a community theater group in Boston.

"And you, you must be my Arkadina, my leading lady," Gary pronounced.

Though flattered and interested, I demurred. "I'm not sure if I could manage my full time job at the Canadian Consulate—I'm the Political and Economic Officer there—and have time for all that would be involved, all the rehearsing and the performances." But I promised to let him know, then more or less forgot about his offer upon arriving at my daughter's.

I had come to help her pack up and move to New York and promptly set to work boxing up her many books. One fell out from a stack of paperbacks I was taking off the shelf. It was a copy of Chekhov's *The Sea Gull*! This was a sign! Now how could I refuse to take the part? I could not, so I joined the cast. We rehearsed nights and weekends throughout a very cold winter, sometimes in unheated spaces warmed only by the fire of our emoting and eventually performed the play in the spring, to some acclaim.

Shortly after The Fenway Players' performance, another *Sea Gull* landed on stage. It was a production of the Chekhov Film and Drama Company, a group affiliated with Boston University. When I learned that the director, a Russian emigre, was taking the company abroad to perform in a Chekhov drama festival in Yalta and later in St. Petersburg, I persuaded him to let me audition as a stand-in for the role of Arkadina, a role I was perfectly ready to play.

"And I'll help with any backstage work, or anything else you might need an extra set of hands for," I promised. I really wanted to make this trip, and believe this offer helped convince him to let me join the company.

I never got to go onstage because that Arkadina never missed a performance. But I was happy with my role as a general factotum and gofer. I stitched up ripped costumes and pressed them, helped to cue the music, ran errands and was dispatched daily, when in St. Petersburg, to the local open-air market for lunch makings. Best of all, I had the opportunity to travel through Russia, a country I could finally visit.

En route to Yalta, we stopped over in Helsinki giving me an

opportunity to visit the original Marimekko store and purchase a dream dress and a few other signature items. It's just as well that both my suitcase space and budget were severely limited or I would have been tempted to buy more. From there we flew to Kiev where we had a tour of that grand city with its imposing gates and basilicae. Then on to the train station, where our bedraggled troupe waited with suitcases and scenery for the train to Simferopol, in Crimea. And waited and waited. Finally, we realized we were on the wrong platform. Attempting to cross a stretch of five tracks to reach the right place was sheer idiocy, but it's what we did, tripping, dropping bags, nearly losing everything in the process, and risking the appearance of a train chugging into the station on one of the tracks.

Eventually, we reached the right platform only to discover that our director was missing and had boarded the wrong train, the one going in the opposite direction, the one we sprinted away from. So we waited some more, trusting that he would catch a train back. Hours went by. In the raw April weather, in our light jackets and raincoats, we were chilled to the bone. At long last, we were reunited and on our way once more. In Simferopol, we all boarded a bus to Yalta.

There we were lodged in a home for actors, a place where Russian actors could retire or stay during a performance. It was located in a beautiful spot on the Black Sea, surrounded by early blooming bushes and blossoming fruit trees. The city itself, like an aging dowager, still retained vestiges of beauty, run down though it was. A funicular ride gave a sweeping view of the city and coastline. On the promenade along the water's edge, I couldn't resist buying caviar from strolling peddlers; I bought cornflakes and sundries at a local market. Several of us hiked around in the amazing Nikitsky Botanical Gardens not far from the city and marveled at its special treasures, among them a thousand year old pistachio tree and an area known as the "Citrus Cape" where frost-resistant oranges and lemons grow.

Of course, we trooped up to the site where Roosevelt, Churchill, and Stalin held their Yalta Conference in February of 1945. I stood at the end of the long, polished table where these three leaders sat when deciding the future of the war-torn world and tried to imagine the enormity of the power they wielded. They divided Germany in two. They settled the fate of Europe.

Europe was already divided between East and West—Yalta was not to blame for that division. But the conference could have united Europe since all three powers had pledged themselves to help any liberated or former Axis satellite states form democratic governments. The Western Allies kept their Yalta promises; Stalin did not. Instead, he proceeded to solidify the takeover of eastern Europe and guaranteed the spread of Communism throughout. Thus began the Cold War.

Back in the theater, our play was well received; performing in English presented no problem since the audience knew the work so well. After our performance, several of us joined the audience to watch the other competing casts present more Chekhov. We were not allowed to take our coats into the theatre, even though it was drafty. I shivered through *The Cherry Orchard* and then, come intermission, several of us headed for the "ladies." I inched along in the line with the rest and, still far from the door, got my first whiff of the facilities. Once inside, the smell almost gagged me. The stalls were disgusting, what with wet seats and floors, and worse, there was no toilet paper. At the one and only sink, there were no towels. Fortunately, we had all been advised to travel with a roll of toilet paper and we did, so the lack of it wasn't too unsettling for us; however, the Russian women, all dressed up for an evening at the theatre, had none at all and, what's more, didn't seem to mind a bit!

One day we made a pilgrimage to Chekhov's home in Yalta, a charming villa set in an inviting garden. For reasons of health, he retired there in 1889 and viewed it as exile because his "warm Siberia," as he designated the Crimea, was so far from Moscow, the center of the theatre for which he wrote. The interior of his home is kept as it was when the good doctor lived there. I had the feeling he would appear at any moment, adjust his glasses and take his tea.

After a week in Yalta, we returned to Simferopol to board a train for the thirty-six hour journey to St. Petersburg, where we would spend two more weeks. We were billeted four to a compartment in the second class coach—I drew an upper berth—and passed the time playing cards, singing, saying lines, and struggling with rudimentary Russian vocabulary words. We watched the endless countryside fly by. Forests, plains, villages and vast empty spaces came into view. We ate our packed provisions, which would have to last for several meals since there were only tea and vodka available on board.

Performing one's ablutions, though, was the real challenge. The WCs were cesspools: urine on the floors, scum in the sinks, cold water only. The stench was overwhelming.

The trick was to balance on one's heels while maneuvering onto the toilet, then, turning to the sink, attempt to brush teeth while not breathing through the nose and using as little as possible of one's precious bottled water. One emerged gasping and feeling grungier than upon entering. This was the time for a shot of vodka.

The wonders of St. Petersburg erased all unpleasant experiences of getting there. Here our company was sponsored by the Mayor's Office of Culture and Tourism. We were housed with Russian hosts and took our main meals at an arts center. I was pleased to be the guest of a woman who had been an opera singer. She could speak no English and I no Russian, but she had studied German in school so we managed to communicate in that language. I did attempt some Russian phrases, with no great success, and was grateful that she agreed to my using *Frau* rather than the more cumbersome and rather archaic title *Gospozha* when calling her by name. Each of us had brought along from the U.S. such treasured items as soap, deodorant, nylons, and so forth for our hosts and knew these items would be most welcome. *Frau* Olga was, in fact, delighted with my offerings.

I bought a bag of oranges for her, too, but she chided me for spending too much. This was 1993 and a market economy was making itself felt but while the shops were full of goods, everything was expensive. Nonetheless, she served coffee for me at breakfast, a special treat given its cost. She also prepared hot milk for the cold cereal I lugged along from Yalta! There was beet sugar and kasha, a buckwheat porridge, and even red beet borscht for breakfast. To accompany the meal, my host turned on the television and we watched a Latin American soap opera, in Spanish with subtitles in Russian. *Frau* Olga was a devotee of this popular program and apparently never missed an episode. I got sort of hooked, as well, even though I couldn't understand either the spoken or written dialogue—but there was a lot of action and emotion to hold my attention.

The morning of April 12, *Frau* Olga skipped her soap to watch ceremonies commemorating the anniversary of Yuri Gagarin's flight into space; it was on that date in 1961 that the cosmonaut became the first man in space—for all of one hundred eight minutes! *Frau* Olga was so proud of this record, and rightly so.

There was also borscht for lunch, and often for dinner. I really liked it but was not prepared for the consequences of too much borscht and thus was startled to discover how red the water in the toilet bowl had become. Upon comparing notes with my fellow travelers, I learned they, too, were suffering from the red borscht blues.

Thank goodness my hostess escorted me the first time I descended into the bowels of the earth to ride the subway. The escalators run so far down I wondered if I would ever surface. But it proved to be a clean, fast and safe ride so I continued to use the subway for long distance traveling. Upon emerging, I would join the jostling crowds along the *Nevsky Prospekt*, or walk down to the Neva to watch the ice floes float by.

The troupe was taken on several tours of the city, and, of course, to the Hermitage where, in the Winter Palace, we saw but a small selection of the marvels on exhibit there. I recall the lavish and magnificent setting of the interior—gold leaf, malachite, jasper, and marble provided the backdrop for all the art treasures. I remember gazing upon the beautiful *Litta Madonna* by da Vinci, sometimes called the *Blue Madonna* (wrongly, I was informed by our guide), and Titian's martyred *St. Sebastian*. We were also able to visit the private theater of Catherine the Great within the Hermitage and each of us, in turn, sat in the seat she always occupied at her command performances.

There was an excursion west of the city to Petrodvoretz, a stunning complex built by Peter the Great on the Gulf of Finland. Here was his villa, Monplaisir, and a whole series of palaces built in addition, all set within a spectacular ensemble of gravity-powered fountains, the site's main attraction. The uncontested centerpiece of all was the Grand Cascade and Water Avenue, a symphony of fountains and cascades. The focal point of the Grand Cascade is an heroic statue of Samson rending open the jaws of a lion, a symbol of Peter's victory over the Swedes. Alas, we had to use our imaginations to envision such splendor for the fountains, destroyed by the Nazis during World War II, were shut down for restoration. Nonetheless, one could tell from the layout and sketches and the on-going construction how breathtaking the site would be in operation.

In St. Petersburg, our company performed Shakespeare—*Hamlet*—as well as Chekhov and, in between my lunch runs to the market and backstage tasks, I had time to shop—in the kiosks of the underground and in the arcades and on the street. The street vendors were the most interesting, displaying true entrepreneurial spirit. Men and women hawked all kinds of wares from rubber tires and books to milk, eggs, and chickens, and almost anything else one could want. I paused in wonder before one seller. The man was holding out both arms over which were hung, by their straps, brassieres in many colors and sizes! Some were huge and I simply had to examine such devices. As I fingered one sample, he nodded approvingly and exclaimed, "*Bolshoi, bolshoi!*" ready to detach it for me. I certainly was not that "big" and hastened to correct him. "*Nyet, nyet: maly, maly,*" small, I explained, whereupon he stared at my chest and tried to judge for himself. I started to laugh since he obviously couldn't divine my size given the layers of clothing I had on to keep out the cold. Then he started to laugh and we both stood there laughing, enjoying the joke together.

After that encounter, I decided to try an indoor shopping arcade where I hoped to find a fine icon to take home. Unfortunately, the icons on display were just recently made and I learned that no antique ones were for sale, nor could they be taken out of Russia even if acquired. I stood peering into the display case, seeing nothing I would be happy with when I became aware of someone standing near me. A young man in a long overcoat, looking studious with his glasses and short beard, leaned in and asked in understandable English, "You wish to buy icon?"

"Yes, but it's not possible to buy an old one," I replied, hoping to convey my disappointment.

"Ah, but I have antique icons to sell!" He moved some distance from the counter and I followed.

I brightened, and, forgetting how I would get home with an antique icon, I asked where they were.

"At my home," he replied. "You come there with me now? Is not far."

Oh, no, thought I. "Can you please bring some here for me to see?"

He could and would so we arranged to meet again in the nearby stairwell. I waited about a half hour, passing the time roaming through the arcade admiring the cases of amber jewelry, the Matryoshka dolls within dolls, Babushka "grandmother" scarves, fringed shawls in a multitude of designs, paintings, and more until he reappeared carrying a package under his arm.

He had brought three beautiful icons. I chose one showing an angel flanked by the two Marys—Mary the mother of Jesus and Mary Magdalene. Above the angel appeared a small face of Jesus. Each figure wore a halo of gold that glowed. The colors of the garments were vivid and appropriate: the angel in white, Jesus's mother in dark red and blue, and Mary Magdalene in pale blue and rose. Their features were distinct and slightly different, one from the other. The icon was painted on a block of wood that was punctuated by tiny wormholes. My dealer presented a certificate of authenticity that accompanied the icon. Though it was written in Russian and I couldn't verify it, I liked the icon so much I decided to buy it. For $40.00 U.S. dollars it was mine. I'd worry later about how to get it out of the country.

The Culture Ministry, our sponsor in St. Petersburg, planned many events for us. A most memorable one occurred on the Eastern Orthodox Easter Sunday. Our group visited St. Isaac's Cathedral, the largest of the mid-19th century domed edifices and the most grandiose. Its interior contains massive granite columns, outstanding sculpture, valuable paintings and highly prized mosaics. But for me, the most impressive art works were the screens of stately icons, through which the priests would come and go, chanting and offering prayers and the host to the crowd of parishioners. We were all standing for there were no pews or chairs and the cold of the marble floors seeped into my thin soled shoes but that discomfort could not diminish my appreciation for the beauty of the church and the gratifying realization that Russians could worship again

Another special occasion was a reception held in a large, imposing room of a Ministry building. There was dancing and a table laden with delicacies—caviar, pâté, a ham decorated to resemble an egg, cucumbers in sour cream, mushroom pickles, almond mazurka, and paske (a cheese-egg dessert, I was told) to name but a few of the tasty delights of the smorgasbord.

During the dancing, I met Evgeny, a Russian businessman who was a close friend of Victor's, the Ministry's representative and our host. Evgeny subsequently appeared at many of our activities and sought me out. He was most attentive and I enjoyed his company, but was focused on seeing the sights. Specifically, I was debating about taking a trip on the midnight express to Moscow the day before our departure for the U.S. Though I had what I calculated would be enough rubles, I had only $25.00 U.S. left and wasn't sure that would be sufficient to get me to Moscow and back and then home.

I procrastinated so long about taking the trip that I was not able to get a second class ticket so I could share a compartment with my colleagues. Instead, I bought a first class ticket. Leaving the ticket office, I looked carefully in both directions, having been warned often of the propensity of Russian drivers to career through the streets. The coast was clear. I stepped into the street and started to walk across when suddenly, out of nowhere, a small car came barreling along. I barely had time to take a step backwards, scarcely managing to keep my feet out from under the wheels, and fell down hard but thankfully managed to avoid being run over! The car did not stop, but several people gathered around me and one woman was hollering for an ambulance. Dear God! I certainly did not want to wind up in a Russian hospital, so to show I wasn't hurt, I staggered up and hobbled, with help, across the street. I guessed I could still make it to Moscow.

The express train was due to arrive around 7:00 a.m. in Moscow. Before midnight, I joined my friends in their compartment until we were underway, then found my own compartment and went right to bed. The sleeper was clean and neat, such a contrast to the coach we took from Ukraine. I undressed and removed the passport/money pocket I wore around my neck and tucked it under the edge of my pillow. I set my travel alarm clock and slid closed the latch at the top of the door, just as the conductor had showed me to do. I was soon lulled to sleep by the gentle swaying of the car. The train made brief stops that roused me slightly, but the renewed motion rocked me right back to sleep.

I awoke again, disturbed this time by light coming into the compartment. Were we already in Moscow? I strained my eyes and was startled to see the light wasn't coming from the window, covered with its dark shade, but from the door, which was slanted open a crack. How could this be? I had locked the door from the inside! I lay stiff and still. I heard a faint rustling coming from below. I heard sounds like the shuffling of paper. I felt carefully and silently under my pillow: no money pouch there! I tried to glance down without turning over and from the corner of my eye I made out a dark figure stretched along the floor for the length of the berth! My heart was beating like a drum but I didn't hesitate. I immediately leaped on top of the figure, sitting on his butt and pounding him on the back and head with all my strength. And screaming, "Stop, stop thief!" He was probably stealing my passport as well as my money. Omigod, maybe he was armed! We had been told never to get into a cab alone—Americans had been killed after being robbed in their taxis and then were dumped along the roadside. Just as I realized I could be asking for real trouble, the figure squirmed and bucked, throwing me off, and ran out the door.

I hastily pulled on my ankle high boots and lit out into the cold corridor after him, clad only in my thin white Victoria's Secret nightgown, yelling the while, not knowing what he took, but not wanting him to get away. I caught up with a figure fighting with the door at the end of the car and grabbed him by the pants, yanking them down—with his pants around his ankles, he couldn't move, I figured.

"Gotchya," I yelled triumphantly. But the man, who turned out to be another American, yelled back, "It's not me! It's not me!" as he whirled around, affording a full frontal view before pulling up his pants—a small distraction in my distress.

He was, in fact, the guy from the compartment next to mine. My screams had awakened him and he discovered that he had been robbed of some $50.00 U.S. He explained his loss as we struggled to get the door to the next car open, after having checked the WC where the robber could have ducked in to hide—if he wore a gas mask, that is.

So through the next car we ran. It occurred to me that my friends were in that car, but there was not a sound from them, despite our calls for help. Up to the third car we raced but could not budge the door at the end of that car. My fellow victim picked up the samovar that was sitting in the corner of the corridor and bashed out the window of the door. We got the door open and pushed through. There was no sign of the robber, instead there stood outside his compartment a discombobulated Dutchman whose hastily donned trousers were held up unevenly by suspenders over his bare chest. He had no shoes on. He had been robbed of hundreds of his German marks. The three of us must have made quite a comical-looking posse on our Keystone Cops-like chase through several more cars, finding no trace of the thief! Fortunately, there were no more victims, either.

Finally, a conductor appeared. He seemed to ask what was wrong. As if he didn't know! I demanded, in no-nonsense English, that we be taken to the train master. The Dutchman was seemingly seconding this. My fellow American agreed. Our attitude, if not our ultimatum, must have been understood, for the conductor motioned for us to follow him.

We marched through a couple more cars and into the train

master's compartment, a small, stifling hot space smelling of tobacco and drink. The man managed to suppress a grin as he looked us up and down. At least he didn't laugh outloud, for there we stood, I in my nightie and boots, the other American in jeans and loafers, the Dutchman sporting suspenders and bare feet—a threatening trio indeed! He heard us out, in two languages he probably didn't understand, but he didn't seem the least bit surprised at our tirade. He undoubtedly knew what we were complaining about. However, it was clear from whatever he was saying that there was nothing he could or would do. Then, as we stood there, still shivering despite the heat and waiting for some satisfactory response, he simply shrugged. His expression had changed from suppressed amusement to annoyance. He took another swig of vodka and waved us away. And that was that.

As we straggled back to our respective compartments, we wondered where the robber could have disappeared. We had checked toilets but we couldn't check the conductors' compartments, so we deduced that the thief could have knocked on one of those doors and found refuge. As I was sifting through my ransacked belongings scattered on the floor, I discovered that he had taken only my U.S. dollars. I still had my passport, thanks be, and my rubles. A credit card was also there, as was my jewelry that I had put on the pull-down shelf. There came a knock on my door. I opened it a crack and saw my car's conductor. He came in to offer what I took to be his apologies. He seemed sincere. He made a note of my loss and helped me double check what remained. But there was no way any of my money would be recovered.

In the morning, my friends told me they heard all the goings-on, but were afraid to see what it was. My response was a bit sarcastic. However, they lent me sufficient dollars to get me back to

Boston and I set out to see Moscow on my limited rubles. I toured the enormous Red Square; gaped at Lenin, a yellowing relic of the past, lying in his tomb; strolled through the GUM store with its multitude of shops and merchandise ranging from fabulous fur coats to foods; admired the multicolored grandeur of the 16th century St. Basil's Basilica of the Blessed, stumbling over all the uneven stone steps inside its marvelously intricate interior; then, back outside, I gazed in awe at that formidable fortress, the Kremlin, headquarters of the erstwhile enemy.

Hungry, I made a beeline for the Moscow McDonald's, just a couple of blocks away. It was a very popular choice. After standing for a long time in a long line, I devoured my hamburger and fries. It was a welcome taste of home and I silently blessed McDonald's policy of standardization. I had been unable to find a seat and found myself standing at a counter next to a man, clearly an American, who turned out to be a bodyguard hired to watch over a group of high school students traveling to Russia from Seattle. He said he had been on duty all night during their trip to Moscow on the midnight express. And he had the answer to my robbery!

He related how he had seen a man board at one of the stops, get a step stool from a conductor and instructions where travelers with hard currency were billeted, and, armed with the proper screwdriver, climb up to loosen the top latch on the doors from the outside of the selected compartments, enabling them to be opened. So the train personnel were in cahoots with the thieves and my own conductor no doubt profited. So much for his solicitousness. The bodyguard said he had tackled the guy he spotted, keeping the students safe, but the thief got away to rob again, or there were others like him. However, at last I knew how my misfortune had been managed.

Later, I met my friends so we could go together to visit the cemetery where Chekhov is buried. After a long streetcar ride, we arrived at the Novodevichy Monastery within whose white walls the cemetery is located. With the help of a plot map and some luck, we found the grave. Surrounded by a lacy, waist-high wrought iron fence and sheltered by a large tree nearby, there stands a narrow stone monument shaped like a cottage, complete with an A-line roof and stylized chimneys. A plaque announces Chekhov's statistics. The serene setting gave the impression that the playwright was back in his own country place, in Yalta, just resting till tea time.

We wandered around on our way out, passing Khruschev's plot. Between two massive blocks of stone, one white and one black and carved in irregular shapes, there appears his large head, peering out of one of the cut-out portions. One could imagine that Khrushchev is standing there between the pillars. The monument was designed by Ernst Neyoestny, a sculptor whom Khrushchev had once denounced for promoting "degenerate art." The irony is delicious.

Shostakovich's grave is also in this cemetery. It is bounded by a low, plain wrought-iron railing. His is a spare stone that bears a special musical notation. Since most of the composer's works carry a key signature, notes he used as a personal monogram in his scores, it is these notes that appear in a single measure on his headstone: D, E flat, C, and B. They make a fitting tribute to Russia's preeminent composer.

Amid all the oversize statuary in the cemetery, one especially stood out, that of a bemedaled Russian general, standing larger than life and speaking into a stone telephone that trailed a remarkable stone cord snaking up from statue's base! I couldn't help but think he was calling God, beseeching Him, perhaps, for forgiveness, for a last minute reprieve. Our pilgrimage complete, we rode back, in solemn mood, to Red Square.

After a bite to eat, an insubstantial substitute for dinner since I was almost out of rubles, I walked to the station and bought a second class ticket for the return trip to St. Petersburg. Fortunately, I could now share a sleeping compartment with my fellow travelers. We barricaded ourselves inside and put chewing gum around the top of the door, in addition to latching it. The gum seal seemed to make us feel safer even though it was strictly cosmetic for I knew no thief would be interested in second class passengers. And sure enough, we arrived back undisturbed and not too much the worse for wear.

Now it was time to leave St. Petersburg. It took me quite a while to get ready for the journey home. I had to devise some way to smuggle the icon out of Russia for I knew it couldn't be packed in my suitcase where it could easily be discovered. Bad enough that I had to pack the caviar, a large tin of which I had bought on the black market in Yalta. That I could give up if I had to, but I certainly did not want my icon confiscated or, worse, have to face charges for trying to leave the country with a forbidden article. My friends, sworn to secrecy about my planned caper, said they would disown me if I were arrested. I'm sure they meant it and I understood that. This was my risk alone.

I had acquired several plastic bags during my stay and, as I wrapped up some small items, I automatically put the icon in one. Then it hit me! I could attach that bag to my bra straps, layer myself in extra clothing and get the icon through customs undetected. Surely customs would not perform a body search. So, with safety pins and knots, I managed to affix the icon bag. It had to hang above my waist, or I couldn't sit, but it couldn't be too close to my neck, either. So, I wound up with the 7"x 5" block of wood directly over my bosom. It really didn't stick out that much, being only one inch thick. Then, on came a blouse, two sweaters and my raincoat and no one could tell what I was hiding. True, I looked a bit busty and would have to sit up straight and not breathe too deeply, but I felt this would not present a problem.

After affectionate goodbyes to *Frau* Olga, my hospitable hostess, I was surprised to see that Victor had come to pick me up in his car. Well, I thought, this would be a much better ride than bouncing along on the bus I was expecting to be crammed into. Victor opened the door to the back seat, and there was Evgeny! I was quite surprised to see him, too. On the way to the airport, he spoke of his newly launched computer business, but with little enthusiasm.

"It's wonderful that you have started up your own company," I ventured. "How do you like being a 'capitalist'?"

"I am not sure. It does not satisfy Russian soul." He did not seem happy.

As we approached the airport, he gave me a letter to mail to his cousin in Chicago and I assured him I would. I emerged with some difficulty as he helped me out of the car. I held out my hand to bid him goodbye when he suddenly took me in his arms and kissed me on the mouth. He held me so tight I could hardly breathe. I can only wonder what he must have been thinking as he pressed me to his chest. Perhaps that I had wooden implants! Maybe the sweaters cushioned the crush for him; as for me, the block was cutting into my breasts and I was gasping for air. As he walked away, he turned to wave but did not smile back as I blew him a kiss.

I grabbed my suitcase and joined the line that was winding towards the airport entrance. No wonder we had arrived so early. It would take a long time to clear customs, I was sure. As time

wore on, I became anxious. Finally, after waiting for a little over
two hours, I got inside and could observe the set up. There were
five counters positioned like check-out counters at a supermarket.
Each counter was staffed with two customs officials who were
searching through suitcases. The checkers stood sideways to me
and I could observe which ones were the most thorough, which
more lax. As I surveyed the prospects, my eyes fastened on the
counter where two women were gabbing away while giving the
bags a cursory look. That's where I wanted to go through, to save
my caviar, not to mention my nerves, but those checkers were
busy with another passenger when it came my turn to approach.
The official in charge of the traffic flow motioned me to the
counter that was now free but I did not want to be at the mercy of
the two officious-looking men there who were unloading everything from the cases they examined.

Fortunately, I remembered a bit of tradecraft from my spy
days: create a diversion.

I moved forward clumsily and dropped my purse, spilling its
contents over the floor. The "traffic cop" gave me a disgusted look
and waved me along to the next person. I dropped to my knees
and scooped up my belongings as quickly as I could, given my
impediment, and finished just in time to get to the two women,
whom I greeted in a friendly, flustered fashion. They were most
sympathetic and gave my suitcase a quick going-over, without
finding the caviar. I received their clearance stamp and was con-
gratulating myself when I realized that there loomed another
checkpoint ahead: the metal detector. Surely the gold leaf on the
icon wasn't enough to set it off. Surely the metal detector wasn't
sensitive enough to pick up the gold leaf. I looked beyond the
detector and saw that the troupe had made it through and there
they all stood, waiting to see what would happen to me.

My turn was fast approaching. I tried to take a deep breath but thought better of it. I was wearing my rings and watch and my belt with a metal buckle. Should the alarm sound, I would have a second chance to go through after removing those articles, and could still hope the icon would not set it off again. I stepped forward. After two more steps I had sailed through. The detector had not made a sound. Hallelujah! My audience was relieved, too, and, fortunately, did not clap at my safe emergence—something that certainly would have drawn attention to my passage. That's one performance I didn't want recognition for.

Together again, we all waited, standing up, for a long time in a sort of holding area before we finally boarded the plane. Once on board, I adjourned to the lavatory and removed my precious block of wood, breathing much easier, literally and figuratively. The icon now occupies a prominent place in my living room, high up on a shelf at the top of a built-in bookcase. From there, Jesus and the others seem to be smiling down on me.

The year following our visit to Russia, the Office of Culture in St. Petersburg sent some of its actors and entertainers to Boston. Victor, the city's representative, accompanied the group, and brought me a message from Evgeny. It was, rather, an invitation to return to St. Petersburg as his guest during the White Nights of June the following summer! Victor gave me Evgeny's phone number and I promised Victor I would consider the trip and let Evgeny know.

I was tempted to go, but later that year I lost my job and was preoccupied with finding another. At Christmas time, I sent Evgeny a card, in care of Victor, and added a note explaining my situation but saying I was still thinking about coming if I could manage it. I gave him my phone number and also asked him to write. By the end of January, I hadn't heard from him and finally phoned. The telephone was evidently in a hall, for another resident in the building answered and became hysterical when I asked for Evgeny. I couldn't understand her reaction and decided to call Victor's home. I spoke with his wife, Yelena. She told me that Evgeny had committed suicide the week before! I was stunned! No wonder the woman on the telephone had become so upset at my call.

Yelena said that Evgeny's company had gotten into serious trouble and he had also been enmeshed in a nasty divorce. He had become terribly despondent.

"Oh, Yelena, this is dreadful! I am so sorry. I feel awful. Didn't Victor get the Christmas card I sent to him for Evgeny?"

"Victor never mentioned a card. He changed offices and mail must have gotten mixed up. I'm sure he did not receive it."

"Oh, no! So Evgeny never knew I wrote, never knew I might have come over."

"No, he didn't. I'm so sorry, Shirley. He spoke of you often. I know he had hopes of seeing you again."

Maybe hope is not enough. This still makes me sad and I shall always wonder whether, if he had received my card, it would have made a difference. I know I shall always regret not having phoned him earlier.

7

Lifelines

The only thing constant in life is change.
—La Rochefoucauld

*I*t was October of 1999. The remnants of hurricane Floyd roared into Boston in the form of rain—unrelenting, wind-driven rain. Sheets of rain pelted the city and flooded the streets for almost three whole days. It was not safe nor smart to go outside. It was, of course, the very days of my move out of Boston to the "sunny South."

I watched my piano sway in the wind and the wet as it was lowered out of the window of my third floor condo. I tried not to think of the effects of storage on my saturated belongings. At last the condo was emptied, the moving van was full, and all that remained was to clean up the place, load up my car with my clothes and favored plants and drive away the next day, headed for Oxford, MS. How could something that seemed so easy become so difficult to do? Because I lived on one of the narrow, no-parking streets of Beacon Hill.

That hadn't bothered me at all until I became a car owner, right before my departure. But now I needed to park directly in front of my building. I couldn't park even a block away because I couldn't carry my clothes any distance during the deluge. I thought I was quite smart to have saved the signs that were issued to me for blocking off space for the moving van. In the pelting rain, I placed them in position and parked between them. I made two successful loading-up trips but the signs obviously weren't meant to exempt my car, for by the time I came out with another load of clothing, I found a sopping wet ticket on the windshield.

There was no I way I could move the car so I went back upstairs to collect the last load of things. By the time I descended with my final armload, there was another $30 ticket curled around the wiper. Instead of sweeping up the condo as I had planned to do before driving off, I decided I couldn't risk getting yet a third ticket. So I drove off, fuming. I took my overnight bag to the hotel where I had a reservation for the night and headed for a parking garage. Car parked and contents locked safely inside, I set out for the walk through the Public Garden back to the condo. But, as I neared the garage exit I realized I didn't have my umbrella, and knew it was not in the car. It was, in fact, back in the condo where I had thoughtfully left it out and then left without it in my haste to move the car. There was no chance of finding a cab in the downpour, so I had no choice but to slog across town, anger with myself and the meter maids mounting as my feet squished in my sneakers and hair stuck to my face. I reached the condo cold and soaked to the skin.

Inside it was warm, so off came my clothes and went straight into the dryer—even the sneakers. I took up the broom and swept through the rooms stark naked—a liberating dance of departure on the eve of retirement but, oh, how hard it was to leave this place I had so happily called home!

As I wiped off the windowsills one last time, I could see the geraniums still blooming in the window boxes even though it was late fall. I thought of how the wide windows let in the filtered sun that shone so softly on the pale yellow walls. I envisioned the fire in my fireplace, casting flame's gentle glow on the silver Paul Revere bowl that had sat on the coffee table along with the beautiful art books—my coffee table books—I hadn't had the chance to savor satisfactorily. Certainly retirement will bring time to do just that, I reasoned, yet this move marked a sea change, presenting possibilities, of course, but also requiring a leap into the unknown.

I remembered the wrench of leaving my childhood home in Illinois for Washington, D.C., and the job that eventually took me to Europe. I still remembered the wave of *Heimweh* that overtook me for a while when first starting my government assignment in Vienna, Austria. The gray days of my first winter there made me feel even more forlorn. The homesickness soon abated though, thanks in no small part to the weekly letters from home. The newsy, solicitous, loving letters from Mother with a postscript from Dad, complete with his signature drawing of a stickman, the figure he always drew for me as a child, cheered me enormously. They reassured me that all was well at home, that even though my life had become quite different, nothing else had changed. I think this realization, that things were the same back home, gave me the courage to continue on my own and their letters connected me to all that was familiar and far away. It was as if those words, side by side, were strung into a strong, slender strand and cast across the ocean to rescue me—a life line to anchor me safely to the other side.

I had saved some of those letters, now treasured words from loved ones gone away on their heavenly journeys. I found them again when packing up, resting near the bottom of a chest that stood at the foot of my bed. I read some of them once more. How everyone came alive through those pages! My mother's clear, open, unrushed Palmer hand tells me once more of my aunt and uncle coming to supper, of the celebration of my grandparents' 50th wedding anniversary and my grandfather's 40th year in the ministry at Zion Lutheran Church in Bethalto. "We all wished you could have been with us, Shirley-girl, but know you couldn't come all the way from Vienna. Grandma loved the shawl you sent and Grandpa began puffing on the Meerschaum pipe right away."

Mother reported on the latest news at the elementary school where she taught.

"Mrs. Fields was caught smoking in the furnace room again! I was the look-out for her but had to run to the cafeteria when three of the boys from the 'big room' started to fight. The principle called her on the carpet and she's a bit angry with me." I was drawn back in time, imagining all those events, remembering their sequels, thinking again of all those who had peopled my past, some long forgotten. Like a safety rope for mountain climbers, these letters link me to each of the dear ones who have gone on ahead.

My recent feelings, however, had been unsettling. So many other transitions I had made without a second thought. When my former husband's employer sent us abroad—several times—I packed up the household and moved without hesitation. But back then, I was not alone. As wife and mother, my family concerns came first and I knew what I needed to do and where I was going. But now I worried and wondered. I called my sister.

"Maybe you should consider moving up here," Marilyn said, "but you're really more of a city girl. You'd hate Vermont." She's right, of course. I am an urban creature and thrive on the sights and sounds and happenings of the city. But shouldn't I now be seeking the "simpler life" in a quieter place?

Earlier, my daughter had phoned from Manhattan to insist upon accompanying me to Florida on a look-see visit I was coupling with a business trip. She didn't want me to make a rash decision on relocating there without a second opinion. I agreed. But first, I was to travel to North Carolina, the headquarters of the pharmacoeconomic company I worked for, and then, on the day after my return, I was scheduled to leave for Tampa.

I was back in Boston and packing for the next trip the following morning but the task was progressing slowly. I didn't feel very well. Soon, I was sick—real sick. I threw some more things in the suitcase and took to my bed. For the rest of the day and through the night, I was up and down and back and forth from bedroom to bathroom. I could only think I had acquired a terrible case of food poisoning—there was no other explanation.

I slept very little and by morning, when I had to rise early to catch the plane, I was sicker still. I had to crawl on all fours to the bathroom and sit on the toilet seat to perform my toilette. Dressing was painful. I wanted to go back to bed, but knew I couldn't. Instead, I called a cab. As I dragged myself and my carry-on out of the condo and onto the street, I realized I didn't have my work materials with me. In fact, I realized that they were not back in the apartment, but at the office. This meant a detour to Charlestown on the way, or rather, out of the way, to the airport.

I couldn't even lift the suitcase into the cab and had to dislodge the driver to do so. I laid down on the back seat and gave him the office address. He didn't know where it was and couldn't read the map he consulted. I had never driven there—always took the "T"— so I was of little help. I summoned enough mental strength to suggest he call his dispatcher, which he did, and we were off. I thought I would throw up as we zigged and zagged and bounced along, taking wrong turns and time outs to get directions again and again.

Once we arrived at the office, I faced several obstacles: getting up the stairs, signing in and wending my way to my cubicle, trying not to look as if I would collapse on the spot. These labors loomed large for I felt so weak and wretched and was perspiring noticeably but I forced myself on. At last, I retrieved my bulging brief case and lugged it back to the cab. By now, I was terribly late for my flight and the cabbie wasn't all that sure how to get to the airport; after several more wrong turns and help from the dispatcher, we finally arrived.

I had only fifteen minutes to get to the gate. No motorized carts were to be seen and it was impossible for me to run, even walk, there so I flagged down a woman pushing a wheelchair and verbally flogged the poor person to power me to the far end of the terminal, where, of course, my gate was located. I made it in the nick of time! The flight was torture. I held the barf bag at the ready, just in case. When we landed, I had to order a wheelchair to take me to the luggage carousel where one lone bag was going round and round—an animal print carry-on—mine—a bag so distinctive I could always identify it without delay. Then came a long, long ride on a shuttle bus across the bay to St. Petersburg and my hotel. I suffered in silence in my seat directly under the air conditioner, next to a heavily perfumed passenger who never stopped talking. I was amazed I didn't throw up!

I managed to check in and stumble to my room where I collapsed on the bed, grateful the ordeal was over. I hadn't eaten all day so I ordered some chicken noodle soup from room service. It came, tepid and too salty to eat. I settled for a coke and fell asleep. I woke up about ten o'clock and made myself get up and get ready to go to bed for good. The little padlock I put on the suitcase was missing and I wondered how it could have come off as I zipped it open, eager to change and end the day from hell. But it was not to be over for I was stunned to see men's underwear inside! My first thought was why any self-respecting man would want to carry animal print luggage? My second thought, that quickly took precedence, was where was my own animal print bag?

There was a name and address in the bag, but no phone number so there ensued many phone calls—to Information, yielding a phone number that didn't answer, and then several frustrating attempts to get through to the airline for help. I had to give up on that pursuit. About 11:30 p.m., I finally reached the fellow traveler who had just gotten home after dining out and was greatly relieved to learn he did indeed have my suitcase—certainly one that looked like it. He hadn't looked at the name tag on the bag when he grabbed it from the carousel and hadn't yet realized that it wasn't his. He promised to bring it to me in the morning, but that was not a satisfactory solution. I explained that I needed my bag now. He, however, was damn sure he wasn't going to plow out at that hour of the night and drive across the bay to return my bag, even though it was his fault for having taken it without checking. It was up to me to get it.

So, I undertook arrangements to retrieve it. It took forever to convince the airport shuttle office to have my bag picked up from him in Tampa and delivered to me in St. Petersburg and, subsequently, for his bag to be returned to him, all of which I would have to pay for. Around 1:30 a.m., there came a knock on my door. The shuttle driver delivered my errant bag and took my money and the man's bag. I put on my pajamas and, exhausted, fell into bed.

Miraculously, I awoke and felt human again. The twenty-four-hour siege was over. I devoured breakfast and spent a productive day on the job. My daughter arrived for the weekend. We looked around St. Petersburg then went on to Sarasota.

I loved the palms and the beaches there, but not the deserted downtown, the touristy shops, the plethora of pickups. We were shown a few condominiums in different locations. All were set in clusters that looked like retirement villages. I envisioned the residents within their individual spaces living separate, air-conditioned lives that converged only around the condo association's pool where they would come together to sit in sagging plastic chairs, sipping and nibbling around the sparkling water. In the spread of the city, there seemed to be no civic center. Everything downtown seemed miles from residential areas. It was a trek to the beach. The tourist places were packed. Sarasota didn't speak to me.

"It doesn't seem right for me," I reported to best friend Shirly.

"But where else do you suggest we look?" she said, as confused as I. She and her husband and I had considered retiring to the same place. It would be so nice to have one friend with whom to start off this new adventure, but I could not count on such comfort. Most likely my connection with those I love would have to be long distance, for I eventually decided to move to Mississippi.

I had found Mississippi, or rather, the state found me. Back in January, in the depths of an especially cold Boston winter when the sidewalks were but single-file paths of ice through shoulder high stacks of snow there arrived in my mailbox an invitation to come to Natchez! What timing! The brochure was decorated with summery scenes of the South and appealed to me immediately. It had no doubt reached my address because I was on a retirement magazine's mailing list, one that could be acquired and used for such pinpoint target marketing. The state was sponsoring a get-to-know-us event that would introduce cities selected as prime retirement centers and the following May I went to see for myself.

There, I learned about the several locations vying for retirees but was especially drawn to the booth Oxford had set up. It displayed the many attractions of the town and featured, first and foremost, its favorite citizen, William Faulkner. Oxford's literary reputation and that of its famous, independent book store, Square Books, made a big impression on me, a would-be writer. But the clincher was the young woman who staffed the booth. Elaine's knowledge of the town, her friendliness and willingness to show me around Oxford on my way back from Natchez convinced me that I would find the town a welcoming and friendly place, and find her a friend in the process.

That visit to Oxford and a subsequent one in July proved me right. Oxford was what I was looking for—an authentic place with a unique and rich cultural heritage, a place where most everyone had lived most of their lives, a place without the artificiality of some of the more familiar retirement destinations. Oxford was large enough to offer the necessities and amenities of life—I didn't need a large city!—and small enough so one could experience a real sense of community, where one could make a contribution and enjoy a feeling of belonging. Maybe there was an unconscious motivation at work as well—along with the lore of the town there may have been the lure of the land near the Mississippi River.

After all, that's the kind of place I came from.

Only after I settled on moving to Oxford did I realize I had a slender, sideways connection to Faulkner: the commonalties of Charlottesville—my having lived there as well, my meeting his daughter and leaving my Doberman with her and my having heard and seen the writer at UVA—all some of life's curious coincidences to be cherished.

Exploring the next layer of contents at the bottom of the chest during that packing-up process, I had made an unexpected discovery: there lay several old, black, three-ring notebooks and suddenly I remembered that these contained the letters I wrote home over many years. Mother had saved them and had given them to me when she moved into smaller quarters. Here I am at college again: "The only period I could get for French is 8:00 on Tue, Thurs, and SATURDAY. Momma, I just hate an 8:00 o'clock class, and on Saturdays to boot!" And from Vienna, after my tonsillectomy: "It was the most awful experience of my life! The doctor made me hold the drip pan myself and I was gagging from the instruments he had down my throat and spitting blood and whatever he had painted my throat with was wearing off and my nose began to run." That episode still gave me chills.

I leafed through the notebook, finding my letters from Luxembourg. I write of canning pickles and tell Mother and Dad of my daughter's ballet recital. "Andrea was so poised and looked so pretty. I had to fix her hair in a French knot that I prayed would not uncoil. It didn't, and she danced divinely! I bought her pink tutu here but had to drive to Nancy, France, for the ballet slippers—pink ones, too. We sat in the first row of the balcony with the American Ambassador and his wife. How about that?"

I needn't have worried that I had never kept a diary—it was a no-no for CIA employees—here was my life in letters, ready to reference when I needed to, had time enough. For I longed to simplify my life, reduce my schedule, and make time for doing so many things I had not had time for—like painting again, writing my memoir, working on my scrapbooks, visiting historic sites, and, of course, seeing my children more often.

I believe it really was fortunate that long distance phoning was a rarity when I lived abroad. At least among my family and friends, phone calls were reserved for events of great moment: a landmark birthday, a dire emergency, or a death. We didn't just call to chat back then; we wrote letters and thanks be for that or I would not have this rich legacy to treasure, to take me back in time.

But now a troubling thought emerged from the crowd of questions colliding in my mind. How shall I stay connected now that the time has come to move away? No one writes letters any more, or rarely does, so there will be precious few handwritten missives to read and re-read, to savor, to save. No more lively summaries of situations, leisurely descriptions, well-constructed sentences, loving closes with, best of all, familiar, recognizable signatures—no more rescuing ropes of words. Will we instead send our messages into cyberspace, flinging them out in hastily typed fragments, replete with typos, to be retrieved in an ugly e-mail format? And, through this medium, will we be presenting a different self to our recipients—a "warts and all" self unadorned by any redeeming turn of phrase, conveying no thoughtful sensitivities and certainly not setting forth words to be preserved for posterity? The prospect is most unsatisfying.

There will be telephone calls, of course, and they will be so welcome. To hear the voices of loved ones will be wonderful, but how

Closures

hard to express one's self fully over the wire—words evaporate in air, call-waiting competes. And yet, will I not want to be linked by whatever the medium with those near and dear to my heart? I shall settle, I suppose, for any kind of connection, for all can be lifelines for me to cling to through the challenging changes to come.

The dryer buzzed, interrupting my thoughts. I put on my warm clothing. The condo was as clean as I could make it. I picked up the umbrella and left, locking the door behind me.

8

Epilogue

Memory believes before knowing remembers.
Believes longer than recollects,
Longer than knowing even wonders.
—William Faulkner

A nother winter was underway. But this one would prove mild for I was now living in the South—in Oxford, Mississippi—in a new location on the eve of a new century. I was confident that my millennium move would bring me welcome new experiences, new friends, certainly warmer weather, and I was right. I was comfortably ensconced in a cozy cottage right off the town Square, already enjoying my new surroundings.

One December afternoon, I was curled up in the big easy chair in front of the television, watching the news. The program was commemorating the "day that will live in infamy," December 7, but my thoughts turned to another anniversary of the same date for it was the day my father died. I suddenly felt far from anything familiar, farther away than ever from my father and mother and wondered, inexplicably, if they knew where I was. Strange, certainly, but the speculation persisted.

I lost interest in the news and looked away, staring blankly through the window at the tall bushes that lined the side of the carport. The foliage was still green. My thoughts drifted to my parents' home in Charlottesville and I saw again the bushes in the back yard and the bird feeder outside the kitchen window. I remembered how Daddy would rig up all sorts of devices in valiant attempts to discourage the squirrels from pirating the birdseed. "Man must be smarter than squirrel," he would declare, refusing to accept defeat even though it became apparent squirrel was outsmarting man.

My father was particularly happy when he saw the cardinals flock to the feeder. That bird was his favorite feathered friend and, being the state bird, the cardinal was plentiful in Virginia, more so even than in Illinois. While I was reminiscing, my eyes caught a sudden movement and from out of nowhere there appeared the biggest, most beautiful red-crested cardinal I had ever seen. I watched, transfixed, as it settled on a branch of one of the bushes and then deliberately turned until it faced the window and looked directly at me! I sat stunned while, in another few seconds, there was a fluttering of wings and a smaller, dove-colored bird flew to the same branch and positioned itself next to its mate so it could look straight at me as well. I gazed back in awe at these unexpected visitors. A male and a female cardinal! A pair, a couple—symbols of my father and mother, heaven-sent!

The birds lingered on their perch long enough for me to absorb the significance of their presence, long enough for me to know I had been found in my new home and long enough for me to know I would never be too far away from those departed ones I loved nor from the power that caused them to come to me.

Acknowledgments

*I*t was a memoir writing course at Harvard and the instructor, Jane Brox, that gave me the encouragement to expand the essays I wrote in class into an actual memoir. Then came my move to Oxford, MS, and work began in earnest. I joined The Novel Group, a book club there, and found a willing audience in its members. My many thanks to those good friends who listened and liked what they heard and urged me on. A very special thanks to Elaine Abadie for her reading of the manuscript and her so welcome ideas and willingness to help me promote the book. Sandra Knispel was enthusiastic about the memoir early on and offered her valuable assistance in publicizing it and her help in reviewing my German. *Vielen Dank.*

From the beginning, my daughter and son were completely supportive and helped me fill in some memory blanks. Andrea made invaluable suggestions on style that I happily incorporated, critiqued my query letters, referred me to writer friends and gave me lawyerly advise; Rob corrected my recollection of certain events, helped me with research on the Faulkner tapes and applied his artistic talents to the cover design and map. My sister, Marilyn, proofed the manuscript and enabled me to finish the project. Their encouragement buoyed me up all along the way; I could not have done this without them.

At a crucial point in the process, I retreated to The Shack Up Inn in Clarksdale, MS, to write without interruption. There, in the Pinetop Perkins cabin, I found renewed inspiration. The walks through the cotton fields, the lovely quiet, the creative essence of the place all combined to spur me on.

A thousand thanks to Heather Riser, head of Public Services at the Special Collections Library at the University of Virginia, and especially to Kathryn Morgan, Associate Director for Special Collections and Head of Collections at the Library. Their assistance in ferreting out the Faulkner tapes and making them available to me was vital.

Joseph Blottner's recollection of Faulkner's days at UVA, in Charlottesville, was extremely helpful and I greatly appreciate the time he took to talk with me.

I am indebted to my cousin David Byrnes for his recollections of his father's experiences in WWII and to my cousin Don Hinrichs for relating the action he saw during the Battle of the Bulge. I am grateful to Daria Dutzmann for her recounting of the divine Russian menu she served at a memorable Easter celebration. To the fabulous Adriana Trigiani for a referral to her agent, my heartfelt thanks. To Bill Hood, for reviewing the espionage sections of my memoir and for his enthusiastic reaction and his referrals, I am so very grateful.

I owe Neil White so many thanks for his generosity that made it possible for me to attend a writer's conference where I received useful feedback and made helpful connections. And for Barry Hannah's faith in me and my memoir, and his recommendations, I shall always be grateful. I so wish he were still here to see it in print.

But *After Many Days* would not be in print were it not for my editor, Harley Patrick, whose invaluable help brought the memoir to life. I can't thank him enough.

About the Author

SHIRLEY PERRY hung up her cloak and turned in her dagger after thirteen years with the CIA. She has had a winning essay published in *The Boston Globe* and has spoken extensively on her intelligence activities and other experiences. She now lives in Oxford, Mississippi.